# The King of Torts

## JOHN GRISHAM

Level 6

Retold by Chris Rice
Series Editors: Andy Hopkins and Jocelyn Potter

**Pearson Education Limited**
Edinburgh Gate, Harlow,
Essex CM20 2JE, England
and Associated Companies throughout the world.

ISBN: 978-1-4082-2114-3

This edition first published by Pearson Education Ltd 2011

1 3 5 7 9 10 8 6 4 2

Original copyright © John Grisham 2003
Text copyright © Pearson Education Ltd 2011
Illustrations by Peter Strucic

Set in 11/14pt Bembo
Printed in China
SWTC/01

The moral rights of the authors have been asserted in accordance with
the Copyright Designs and Patents Act 1988

Published by Pearson Education Limited in association with
Penguin Books Ltd, and both companies being subsidiaries of Pearson PLC

plete list of the titles available in the Penguin Readers series please go to
vely, v        your local Pearson Longman office
rtment, Pearson Education,
ate,           M20 2JE, England.

# Contents

# Introduction

*"Nobody earns $10 million in six months, Clay. You might win it, steal it, or have it drop out of the sky, but nobody earns money like that. It's ridiculous."*

Clay Carter is an overworked, underpaid public defender in Washington, D.C. He is appointed to represent a drug offender, Tequila Watson, who is charged with the apparently motiveless murder of Ramón "Pumpkin" Pumphrey. But while investigating the case, Clay is approached by a mysterious stranger who makes him an offer that he simply cannot refuse. Clay leaves his job and his client. He starts his own law firm and becomes a multi-millionaire by organizing class-action lawsuits—or mass torts, as they are known—against large companies whose products have proved dangerous to the people who have used them. Life seems wonderful—money, beautiful women, invitations to meet the President, private jets, and his picture on the front page of magazines and newspapers across the country—but, as in Marlowe's *Doctor Faustus*, such unlimited financial success and personal pleasure does not come without a price to be paid ...

John Grisham was born on February 8, 1955, in Jonesboro, Arkansas. His father worked as a builder and a cotton farmer, and his mother was a homemaker. As a boy, he dreamed of becoming a professional baseball player but realized that he did not have the talent for this and changed his goals. He was encouraged by his mother to love books, and Grisham soon became an enthusiastic reader. His favorite writer was John Steinbeck.

In 1977, Grisham graduated from Mississippi State University with his first degree, and four years later he graduated from law school. While he was studying law, he was especially interested in criminal and general law, and he made great use of this knowledge in his later work as a writer.

Grisham worked as a small-town general lawyer in Southaven for ten years, and was also elected as a Democrat to the Mississippi House of Representatives in 1983. He was a very busy man, working sixty to seventy hours a week in his law practice, but he still found time for his favorite hobby, writing. In 1984, he began writing his first novel, *A Time to Kill*, which was eventually published in 1988, but at first without great success.

The day after he completed *A Time to Kill*, Grisham started work on a second novel about a young lawyer who worked for a law firm that was not as honest as it seemed. This second novel, *The Firm*, was published in 1991 and was an immediate success. The story was sold to Paramount Pictures for $600,000, and spent 47 weeks on *The New York Times* best-seller list, becoming the best-selling novel of 1991.

After this, Grisham gave up his legal practice and stopped his political work to become a full-time writer. He produced at least one book a year, most of them hugely successful best-sellers. Since *The Firm*, Grisham has written fifteen more legal thrillers, including *The Pelican Brief* (1992), *The Client* (1993), *The Rainmaker* (1995), *The Runaway Jury* (1996), *The Brethren* (2000), *The King of Torts* (2003), *The Last Juror* (2004) and, his most recent book, *The Associate* (2009). He has also written four non-legal novels and one non-fiction book, *The Innocent Man* (2006). Seven of Grisham's stories have been made into movies, greatly increasing his international popularity. The first movie was *The Firm* (1993), with Tom Cruise and Gene Hackman in the leading roles. One of his non-legal stories, *Skipping Christmas* (2001), was made into a movie called *Christmas with the Kranks* in 2004.

In 1998, *Publishers Weekly* announced that Grisham was "the best-selling novelist of the 90s." His books have sold more than 60 million copies worldwide and have been translated into twenty-nine languages. *The Pelican Brief* (made into a film in 1993 with Julia Roberts and Denzel Washington) sold an amazing 11,232,480 copies in the United States alone.

Grisham lives with his wife and two children on their two farms in Mississippi and Virginia.

Almost all John Grisham stories are about law, justice, and the court system. They are always very complicated, showing in great detail the lives of lawyers, judges, and clients, but they are also entertaining and exciting. Honest, ordinary "little" people find themselves in great danger when they fight large, powerful, dishonest organizations. Unlike in the real, modern world, where our lives are increasingly governed and controlled by impersonal, powerful, and often dishonest forces, the "little" person in a John Grisham story usually wins.

*The King of Torts*, however, is Grisham's most unusual legal thriller. In this story, the good guy and the bad guy are the same person. We are given a description of a man, Clay Carter, who finds himself in great moral difficulties. He is basically a decent man who surrenders to his inner greed and becomes a lawyer more interested in making money than serving justice. In this book, Grisham's anger targets the attorneys who work in mass tort litigation. In his view, lawyers like these are damaging the legal profession. Today, in the United States, there is a great debate over changes to tort laws. Grisham's story gives anyone interested in this debate useful information about how these lawyers operate, but it also keeps the reader guessing about how it will all end. How rich is it possible for one man to become before, like Doctor Faustus, he is destroyed by his own greed?

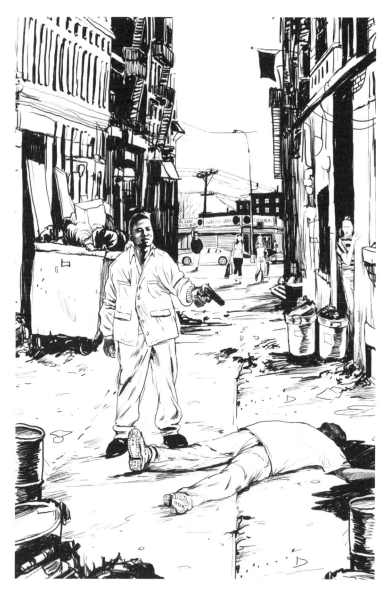

*The shots that fired the bullets that entered Pumpkin's head were heard by eight people.*

## Chapter 1    Tequila Watson

The shots that fired the bullets that entered Pumpkin's head were heard by eight people. Three immediately closed their windows, locked their doors, and withdrew to the safety of their small apartments. Two others, with previous experience of incidents like this, ran away faster than the gunman himself. Another, who was digging through some garbage for cans, jumped behind a pile of boxes until the shooting stopped. Two saw almost everything. They were sitting at the corner of Georgia Street and Lamont Street in front of a grocery store, half-hidden by a parked car so that the gunman, who glanced around briefly before following Pumpkin into the alley, didn't see them. Both told the police that they saw the boy with the gun reach into his pocket and pull it out. A second later they heard the shots, though they didn't actually see Pumpkin get hit. But they *did* see the boy with the gun rush out of the alley and run straight in their direction. He ran bent at the waist with a scared and guilty look on his face. When he passed them he was still holding the gun which, for one terrifying second, he seemed to point at them. Keeping their heads down, both of them crawled as quickly as they could into the grocery store and shouted for someone to call the police— there had been a shooting.

Thirty minutes later, the police received a call that a young man matching the description of Pumpkin's killer had been seen carrying a gun in open view on Ninth Street and acting very strangely. The police found their man an hour later. His name was Tequila Watson, a black male, age twenty, with the usual drug-related police record. No family. No address. The last place he had been sleeping was a rehab unit on W Street. He had thrown away the gun and had also thrown away the cash or drugs he must have stolen from Pumpkin because his pockets

1

were empty. The police were certain that Tequila hadn't been affected by drink or drugs when he shot Pumpkin. After a few quick, rough questions, he was handcuffed, pushed into the back seat of the police car, and taken back to the alley near Lamont Street where he had killed Pumpkin.

"Ever been here before?" one policeman asked.

Tequila said nothing, just stared at the pool of fresh blood on the dirty ground.

After the two witnesses from outside the grocery store had identified him, Tequila was pushed into the car once again and taken to jail. He was charged with murder and sat quietly in a crowded cell, saying nothing to anyone, just staring at the floor.

♦

Pumpkin's mother, Adelfa Pumphrey, was sitting behind a desk just inside the basement entrance of a large office building on New York Avenue, watching the security screens. She was a large woman in a tight brown uniform, a gun on her waist, an empty look on her face. The policemen who approached her had visited her many times before. They gave her the news, then found her boss.

In a city where young people killed each other every day, every mother knew many others who had lost their children, and every mother knew that she could lose hers at any time. The mothers had watched the other mothers survive with horror. As Adelfa Pumphrey sat at her desk with her face in her hands, she thought of her son and his lifeless body being inspected by strangers somewhere in the city at that moment.

She cried for her baby and swore revenge on whoever had killed him.

♦

Adelfa went to court to watch her son's killer being formally charged. The police told her that it would be a quick, routine matter: the killer would plead not guilty and ask for a lawyer. She was in the back row with her brother on one side and a neighbor on the other, crying into a damp handkerchief. She wanted to see the boy. She also wanted to ask him why, but she knew she would never get the chance.

They brought the criminals into the courtroom like cattle at a market. All were black, all wore orange prison suits and handcuffs—and all of them were young. In addition to his handcuffs, Tequila had chains on his wrists and ankles because his crime had been especially violent, though he looked fairly harmless now. Adelfa stared at the thin boy in the orange prison suit and wondered where his mother was, how she had raised him, if he had a father, and—most important—why he had killed her son. The police had told her that drugs weren't involved in the killing. But she knew better. Drugs were involved in every layer of street life.

"Tequila Watson," a court official announced at last.

The prisoner was helped to his feet by another official and moved slowly forward.

"Mr. Watson, you are charged with murder," the judge said loudly. "How old are you?"

"Twenty," Tequila said, looking down.

After the reading of the charge, the courtroom had gone quiet. The other criminals looked at Tequila with admiration; the lawyers and policemen were curious.

"Can you afford a lawyer?"

"No."

"I didn't think you could," the judge said quietly to himself, and looked at the defense table, where usually many PDs, the badly-paid lawyers from the Office of the Public Defender, were waiting to defend the poor. At that moment, however, there was only one: Clay Carter. He had come into the courtroom to pick

3

up a few papers and realized, with horror, that the judge was looking at him.

"Mr. Carter?" the judge said.

Clay swallowed hard. A week earlier, he had finished a murder case which had lasted for almost three years, and he didn't want to defend another one. But he was the only PD in the room, and he couldn't show weakness and refuse to accept a case, especially with policemen and prosecuting lawyers watching. He walked calmly to the bench, took the file from the judge, quickly looked through it, and said, "We'll plead not guilty, Your Honor*."

"Thank you, Mr. Carter. And you'll be this man's lawyer?"

"For now, yes." Clay was already planning to unload this case on someone else at the OPD.

The judge thanked him again and began looking for the next file. Clay, meanwhile, sat next to Tequila Watson at the defense table, and got as much information from him as the young man was willing to give—which was very little. Clay promised to visit the jail the next day for a longer interview; then, grabbing his old, scratched briefcase, he hurried away.

If Clay Carter had ever been attracted to a career in the OPD, he couldn't now remember why. He had been a PD for almost exactly five years and, at the age of thirty-one, he felt tired and exhausted. He was trapped in an office that he was ashamed to show his friends, wanted to leave but didn't know how, and now had another senseless murder case to defend. In the elevator, he cursed himself for his bad luck and stupidity, and promised himself that he would leave and find a better job as soon as he could—the same promise that he had made to himself every day for the last five years.

♦

* Your Honor: formal words of respect used by lawyers when talking to a judge

4

The OPD had eighty lawyers, all working in two small, airless floors of the District of Columbia Public Services Building on Mass Avenue. There were about forty low-paid secretaries and three dozen paralegals scattered around the jungle of tiny offices. The director was a woman named Glenda, who spent most of her time locked in her office because she felt safe in there.

The beginning salary for an OPD lawyer was $36,000. Raises were small and infrequent. The workloads were enormous because the city was losing its war on crime. Like most of the other PDs, Clay Carter had never planned to work for the OPD. When he had been in college and then law school, his father had had a law firm in Washington, D.C. Clay had worked there part-time for years, and had had his own office. The future had looked wonderful in those days, father and son litigating together as the money poured in. But the firm had gone bankrupt during Clay's last year at law school, his father had left town, and Clay had become a public defender. Five years later, he still wondered what had gone wrong.

He threw the Tequila Watson file onto the neat desk in his tiny, windowless office, and wondered how he might unload it onto someone else. He was tired of the tough cases, and all the other garbage that was thrown at him as an underpaid PD. He decided to call Rebecca, his long-time girlfriend, who reminded him that the following day was her mother's birthday. "My parents have invited us both to dinner at the club," she informed him. "Seven o'clock. Coat and tie."

A bad day just got worse. After the short phone call, he stared miserably at Rebecca's photo on his desk and thought he would rather have dinner with Tequila Watson at the jail.

As he was thinking about his four-year romance with Rebecca and how much he hated her rich, aggressive parents, his closest friend at the OPD, Paulette Tullos, appeared in the doorway.

"Bad luck," she said, smiling in the direction of the file on his

5

desk. "Another murder case."

"What are my chances of getting rid of it?" he said.

"Almost impossible. Who are you going to give it to?"

"I was thinking of you."

"Sorry. I have two murder cases already. I heard the prosecutors talking. Another street killing, but no apparent motive."

"There's always a motive—cash, sex, drugs, a new pair of Nikes."

"But the kid has no history of violence."

"First impressions are seldom true, Paulette, you know that."

"Jermaine got a very similar case two days ago. Also no apparent motive."

"I hadn't heard."

"You might try him. He's new and ambitious and, who knows, you might be able to unload it on him."

"I'll do it right now."

Jermaine wasn't in but Glenda's door, for some reason, was slightly open. Clay went in and asked Glenda if she could assign the Tequila Watson case to another PD.

"Who do you want to give it to, Mr. Carter?" she asked him.

"I don't really care. I just need a break."

She leaned back in her chair and began chewing the end of her pen. "We'd all love a break, Mr. Carter, wouldn't we?"

"Yes or no?"

"Move it if you can, but I'm not going to reassign it."

"OK, but what about a higher salary?"

"Next year, Mr. Carter. Next year."

Clay returned to his office to look again at the Tequila Watson file.

♦

They called it the Criminal Justice Center, but it was really just a big jail. A guard led Clay down a hall to a long room divided by a thick sheet of unbreakable glass. He pointed to a chair and Clay sat down and waited for Tequila Watson to appear on the other side of the glass. As he was looking through his papers, the guard whispered in his ear: "Your boy had a bad night. He jumped on a kid at two o'clock this morning and almost beat him to death. It took six of our guys to pull him away. He's a mess."

"Tequila?" Carter was surprised.

"Watson, that's him. He put the other boy in the hospital. Expect additional charges."

"Are you sure?" Clay asked.

"It's all on video."

They both looked up as Tequila was brought to his seat on the other side of the glass by two guards, each holding an elbow. He was handcuffed and, although prisoners usually had their handcuffs removed when they talked to their lawyers, Tequila's handcuffs weren't taken off. He sat down. The guards moved away but remained close.

Tequila's left eye was swollen shut, with dried blood in both corners. The right one was open but it was bright red. There was a bandage around his head and some sticky tape on his chin. His lips and jaw were so swollen that Clay wondered at first whether he had the right client. He picked up the black phone receiver and motioned for Tequila to do the same.

"The police tell me you started a fight with another kid last night and put him in the hospital. Is that true?"

Tequila nodded.

"Did you know the kid?"

"No."

"So why did you attack him?"

"I don't know," Tequila answered, the words slow and painful.

Further questions revealed that the other boy had been asleep when Tequila attacked him for no reason. Clay wrote a few things down in his notebook and looked up again. "They say you killed a boy, shot him five times in the head."

The swollen head nodded slightly.

"His name was Ramón Pumphrey, also known as Pumpkin. Did you know the guy?"

"Yes. I used to buy drugs from him."

"How long ago?"

"A couple of years."

"Did you shoot him?" Clay's voice was almost a whisper. The guards were asleep, but this wasn't a question that lawyers usually asked their clients, especially not at the jail.

"I did," Tequila said softly.

"Five times?"

"I thought it was six."

"Why did you do it? Was it a drug deal?"

"No."

"Girl trouble?"

"No."

Clay took a deep breath. "Do you fight a lot?"

"Not anymore. I had a fight once with Pumpkin when I was twelve years old."

"Did you see Pumpkin often?"

"Not much. Maybe twice a year."

"When you saw him two days ago, did you argue? Help me here, Tequila. I'm working too hard for details."

"We didn't argue."

"Why did you go into the alley?"

Tequila put down the receiver and began moving his head backward and forward, very slowly. He was obviously in some pain. When he picked up the receiver again he said, "I'll tell you the truth. I had a gun and I wanted to shoot somebody. Anybody, it didn't matter. I left the Camp and just started walking, going nowhere, looking for somebody to shoot. When I saw Pumpkin, I took him into an alley and shot him. I don't know why. I just wanted to kill somebody."

"What is the Camp?" Clay asked.

"A rehab place. That's where I was staying."

"How long had you been there?"

"A hundred and fifteen days."

"No drugs or anything for a hundred and fifteen days?"

"That's right."

"Not even when you shot Pumpkin?"

"Not then. Not now."

"Did you ever shoot anybody before?"

"No."

"Where did you get the gun?"

"Stole it from my cousin's house."

"How did you get out of the Camp?"

"After a hundred days, they let you out for two hours."

"So you walked out of the Camp, went to your cousin's house, stole a gun, and shot Pumpkin for no reason."

"That's exactly what happened," Tequila nodded. Then, while Clay was pulling some papers out of his briefcase, he asked, "What's going to happen to me?"

"We'll talk about it later."

"When can I get out?"

"It might be a long time."

## Chapter 2    The Van Horns

Two hours after his conversation with Tequila Watson, Clay parked his Honda Accord directly in front of Deliverance Camp—an old building in a dangerous part of the city just opposite an old gas station where drug dealers regularly did business. He got out and, trying to ignore the curious stares from the young toughs in the sidewalk gangs, walked toward the door. "There's not another white face within two miles of here," he thought as he pushed the bell. After a long wait, during which the young people in the street crowded around him, staring and laughing at him, the door opened and Clay found himself in a large, windowless reception area of cement floors, stone walls, and metal doors. The receptionist showed him into the small, disorganized office of Talmadge X, Tequila Watson's counselor at Deliverance Camp.

Clay showed Talmadge X the documents relating to Tequila Watson's case.

"Did you know about the shooting?" Clay asked when Talmadge X had finished looking at them.

"Not until you called an hour ago. We knew he left on Tuesday and didn't come back. We knew something was wrong, but then we expect things to go wrong. Tell me what happened."

Clay gave Talmadge X the details of what Tequila had told him two hours earlier. When Clay had finished, Talmadge X calmly asked, "What can I do?"

"I'd like to see his file. He's given me his permission."

The file was already lying on the desk. "Later," Talmadge X replied, putting his hand on top of the file. "I need to look at it first. But tell me what you want to know."

Clay wanted to know about Tequila Watson's background, and Talmadge X told him about the boy's mother, who had died when he was three, and his life on the streets, in and out of court and homes for young offenders. He then told Clay about Deliverance Camp: "We get the hard cases, the serious addicts. We lock them up for months. There are eight counselors here, and we were all drug addicts in the past. Four of us are now church ministers. I served thirteen years for drugs and robbery, then I found Jesus. Tequila was on drugs for years. At eighteen, he went to jail for four months for stealing from a shop. Another three months last year for possessing dangerous drugs. Not a bad record for one of us. Nothing violent. But is there anything we can do to help him this time?"

"I'm told there were at least two eyewitnesses. I'm not optimistic."

"Sounds like life imprisonment. But that's not the end of the world for us, you know, Mr. Carter. In many ways, life in prison is better than life on these streets. The sad thing is, Tequila was one of the few who might have succeeded in life."

"Why is that?"

"The kid has a brain. When we got him off drugs and he was healthy again, he felt so good about himself. He learned to read and he liked to draw. I don't understand his motive for this killing, Mr. Clay. Tell me why."

"I can't. *You* tell *me*. You've known him for the last four months. No history of violence or guns. No love of fighting. He sounds like the perfect patient. You've seen it all. *You* tell *me* why."

"I've seen everything," Talmadge X said, his eyes even sadder than before. "But I've never seen this. The boy was afraid of violence. Tequila was one of the weak ones here. I can't believe he'd shoot someone for no reason. And I can't believe he'd jump on a guy in jail and send him to the hospital. I just can't understand it."

There was a long pause, and Clay stood up. "I'll be back tomorrow for the file," he said. "What time?"

"After ten o'clock," Talmadge X said. "I'll walk you to your car."

"It's not necessary," Clay replied, but he was privately delighted with the counselor's offer. When Talmadge X appeared at the door with Clay, the gang of youths scattered in all directions, and Clay was able to drive away unharmed, but secretly fearing his return the following day.

♦

Clay parked his old Honda Accord in a distant lot behind some tennis courts and walked toward the clubhouse of the Potomac Country Club, straightening his tie and complaining angrily to himself. He hated the place—hated it for all the stupid people who were members, hated it because he couldn't join, and hated it because the Van Horns loved it and they wanted him to feel like an outsider. For the hundredth time that day, as every day, he asked himself why he had fallen in love with a girl whose parents were so unbearable. If he had a plan, it was to run away with Rebecca and move to New Zealand, far from the OPD, and as far away as possible from her family.

Bennett Van Horn was absent. Clay said hello to Mrs. Van Horn, wished her a happy birthday, and gave Rebecca a nervous kiss on the cheek.

"Where's Mr. Van Horn?" he asked, hoping he was stuck out of town or, even better, in the hospital with a serious illness.

"He's on his way," Rebecca said.

"He spent the day in Richmond, meeting with the Governor," added Mrs. Van Horn. Clay felt like saying, *You win! You win! You're more important than I am!*

"What's he working on?" he asked politely, trying to sound interested.

"Political stuff," Barbara said. She probably didn't know what her husband and the Governor had been discussing. She probably didn't even know how much her husband had in the bank. She knew what day she played cards with her friends and she knew how little money Clay earned, but most other details were left to Bennett.

A few minutes later Bennett arrived in a rush, full of insincere apologies for being late. He gave Clay a friendly pat on the back, and kissed his girls on the cheeks.

"How's the Governor?" Barbara asked, loud enough for the diners across the room to hear.

"Great. He sends his best wishes. The President of Korea is in town next week and we've been invited to a black-tie party at the Governor's house." This, too, was offered at full volume. He pulled a collection of cell phones from his pocket, lined them up on the table, turned to his daughter and said, "You look tired, honey—a tough day?'

"Not bad."

Rebecca's tiredness was a favorite topic between her parents. They felt she worked too hard. They felt she shouldn't work at all. She was almost thirty and it was time to marry a fine young man with a well-paid job and a bright future so she could have their grandchildren and spend the rest of her life at the Potomac Country Club.

Over dinner Bennett said, with his mouth full, "While I was down in Richmond, I had lunch with my close friend Senator Ian Ludkin. You'd really like the guy, Clay—he's a perfect Virginia gentleman. Anyway, I told him about you—a hard-working, bright young lawyer, Georgetown Law School, a handsome young man with real character, and he said he was always looking for new talent. He said he has an opening for a staff attorney. I said that maybe you'd be interested and I'd tell you about it. What do you think?"

*I think I'm being trapped*, Clay thought. Rebecca was staring at him, watching closely for the first reaction. "That's interesting," he said with some sincerity.

"It's a great position. Fascinating work. Never a dull moment. Lots of long hours, but I told Ian you could do it easily."

"Do *what*, exactly?" Clay asked.

"Oh, I don't know about all that lawyer stuff. But if you're interested, Ian said he'd be happy to arrange an interview. But you'll have to move quickly. A lot of young lawyers like you would really love that job."

"Richmond's not far away," Barbara said.

*A lot closer than New Zealand*, Clay thought. Barbara was already planning the wedding. He couldn't understand Rebecca, Sometimes she felt trapped by her parents, but she rarely showed any desire to get away from them. Bennett used his money as a bribe to keep both his daughters close to home.

"Well, uh, thanks, I guess," Clay said.

"The starting salary is $94,000 a year," Bennett said, lowering his voice for the first time so the other diners couldn't hear.

That was more than double Clay's salary at the OPD, and the Van Horns all knew it. They loved money and never stopped thinking about how to get more of it.

"That's a nice salary," Clay admitted.

"Not a bad start," Bennett said. "Ian says you'll meet the big lawyers in town. Contacts are everything. In a few years, you'll be working in corporate law. That's where all the money is, you know."

Clay didn't reply. He wasn't happy with the idea that Bennett Van Horn was already planning this life for him.

"How can you say no?" Barbara said excitedly.

"Don't push, Mother," Rebecca replied.

"Think about it," Bennett said.

Clay and Rebecca ignored each other for the rest of the meal. The fight would come later. After dinner, Clay thanked Bennett and Barbara for the food and promised to decide quickly on the job in Richmond. When he was certain they were gone, he asked Rebecca to step into the bar for a minute.

"I didn't know about the job in Richmond," she began.

"I find that hard to believe. It seems to me the whole family has been planning this."

"My father's worried about you, that's all."

*Your father's a fool*, he wanted to say. "No, he's worried about *you*. He doesn't want you marrying a guy with no future, so he's going to manage our future for us."

"Maybe he's just trying to help."

"Why does he assume I need his help?"

"Maybe you do."

"I see. Finally the truth."

"You can't work at the OPD forever, Clay. You've been there for five years. Maybe it's time to move on."

"Maybe I don't want to live in Richmond. Maybe I prefer working in D.C. and don't want to be surrounded by a lot of local politicians in Richmond."

Rebecca sat quietly, thinking for a minute. The truth was she did want to stop working; she wanted a husband and family. But she couldn't admit that to Clay.

"I don't care, Clay," she said. "Say no if you want to. Now, I'd like to go."

Clay followed her out of the club, helped her into her BMW, and watched her drive away.

♦

The next day, Clay returned to D Camp to look at Tequila Watson's file, accompanied by Rodney, a career paralegal in the OPD. He felt safer with Rodney, who had grown up on the streets of D.C. and knew them well. Tequila's story was familiar and depressing—drugs, robberies, burglaries, homes for young offenders—but there was a remarkable absence of violence in it. He had never used a weapon to commit a crime. One of Talmadge X's notes in the file read: "He avoids physical violence. He seems afraid of the bigger boys, and most of the small ones, too." According to the file, Tequila behaved well during his stay in D Camp. He seemed to be getting better. But the final entry— Day 115—read: "Allowed out for two hours. Did not return."

Back in the OPD, Clay visited Jermaine Vance, another lawyer, in his small office and compared notes. Jermaine's client was a twenty-four-year-old career criminal named Washad

Porter who, unlike Tequila, had a long and frightening history of violence. As a member of D.C.'s largest gang, Washad had been badly wounded twice in gun battles and had been convicted once of attempted murder. Seven of his twenty-four years had been spent in jail. He had shown little interest in changing his way of life; his only attempt at rehab had been unsuccessful. He was accused of shooting two people four days before the Ramón Pumphrey killing. One of the two was killed immediately, the other was seriously wounded.

Washad had spent six months at Clean Streets, a rehab center similar to D Camp. Jermaine's conversation with Washad's counselor had been very similar to Clay's with Talmadge X. Washad had improved, was a perfect patient, was in good health, was doing well without any drugs, and hadn't had any problems for four months. He was released from Clean Streets in April, and the next day he shot two men with a stolen gun. Jermaine had talked to Washad once, very briefly, in the courtroom while he was being formally charged. "He was in a state of shock," Jermaine told Clay. "He had a blank look on his face and kept telling me that he couldn't believe he'd shoot anybody. He said that was the old Washad, not the new one."

♦

Later that same day, Bennett Van Horn answered one of his cell phones. He was in the Men's Lounge at the Potomac Country Club, whiskey in his hand, playing a game of cards with his friends.

"Clay, how are you?" he said, as if they hadn't seen each other for months.

"Fine, Mr. Van Horn, and you?"

"Great. I enjoyed dinner last night."

"Oh yes, it was really nice. Always a pleasure," Clay lied.

"What can I do for you, son?"

"Well, I want you to understand that I appreciate your efforts to get me that job in Richmond." A pause as Clay swallowed hard. "But truthfully, Mr. Van Horn, I don't really want to move to Richmond. I've always lived in D.C. and this is home."

"You can't be serious," Van Horn said.

"Yes, I'm very serious. Thanks, but no thanks."

"A big mistake, son. You just don't see the big picture, do you?"

"Maybe I don't. But I'm not sure you do either."

"You have a lot of pride, Clay. I like that. But you're making a big mistake—one that could have serious consequences."

"What kind of consequences?"

"This could really affect your future."

"Well, it's *my* future, not yours. I'll choose my next job, and the one after that. Right now I'm happy where I am."

"You're turning your back on a huge increase in salary, Clay. More money, better work. Wake up, boy!"

"I'm not going to argue, Mr. Van Horn. I called to say no."

"You're a loser, Clay, you know that. I've known it for some time. You're a coward with no ambition, no intelligence …"

Clay put the phone down with a smile, proud that he had made the great Bennett Van Horn so angry. He had given him a clear message that he wouldn't be pushed around by stupid rich people like him. He would deal with Rebecca later, and it wouldn't be pleasant.

◆

After an unsuccessful day of trying to discover more about Tequila Watson and Washad Porter, Clay met Rebecca for a drink at Abe's Place, the bar in D.C. where they had first met four years earlier. Rebecca was quiet but coldly determined.

"I talked to my father," she began. "Why didn't you tell me you weren't taking the job in Richmond?"

"Your father called me a loser. Is that what you think, too?"

"I have my doubts."

17

Clay took another drink. This was, in his opinion, almost certainly the end of their relationship, but he didn't want to say anything to hurt her.

"What do you want, Rebecca? Do you want to end it?"

"I think so," she said, and her eyes immediately filled with tears.

"Is there someone else?"

"No. It's just that you're going nowhere, Clay," she said. "You're smart and talented, but you have no ambition."

"That's nice to know. A few hours ago, according to your father, I was a cowardly loser."

"Are you trying to be funny?"

"Why not, Rebecca? Why not have a laugh? It's finished, let's face it. We love each other, but I'm a loser who's going nowhere. That's *your* problem. *My* problem is your parents. They'll destroy the poor guy you eventually marry."

"The poor guy I marry?" Rebecca's eyes flashed angrily.

"Calm down. Listen. I'll make you an offer. Let's get married now. We'll leave our jobs, have a quick, secret wedding, sell everything and fly somewhere far away from here, like the West Coast, and live on love."

"Then what?"

"Then we'll find jobs and start a family. We won't tell your parents anything. But if they find us, we'll change our names and move to Canada."

They both laughed, but the light-hearted moment passed quickly. Briefly, they were reminded of why they loved each other and of how much they enjoyed their time together. There had always been much more laughter than sadness, but things were changing now. Rebecca finished her drink, then she leaned forward and stared Clay directly in the eyes.

"Clay, I really need a break."

"Let's meet in thirty days and discuss it again."

"OK, we'll meet in a month, but I don't expect a change.

This is the end, Clay. You go your way and I'll go mine."

With those words, Rebecca picked up her purse and jumped to her feet. Clay didn't watch her leave, and Rebecca didn't look back.


## Chapter 3   Tarvan


Clay shared a small, two-bedroom apartment with Jonah, an old friend from law school who now sold computers part-time but still earned more money than Clay. The morning after the break-up with Rebecca, Clay was having breakfast and reading the newspaper when the phone rang. He smiled and thought, *It's her. She wants me back already.* But it wasn't Rebecca.

"Mr. Clay Carter," a strange male voice said.

"Speaking."

"Mr. Carter, my name is Max Pace. I work for law firms in Washington and New York. Your name has caught our attention, and I have two very attractive offers that might interest you. Could we meet today?"

"Uh, sure ..." Clay agreed, speechless with surprise.

"Good. Let's meet at the Willard Hotel at noon."

"Noon's fine," Clay said, staring at a pile of dirty dishes in the sink.

Clay put down the phone, wondering whether someone was playing a joke on him. Or maybe it was his father? He had once been a successful lawyer and, although he no longer practiced law, he still had contacts. Maybe he was trying to help his son?

Clay left at eleven thirty and, at the Willard Hotel, was shown up to a room on the ninth floor. The door opened and Max Pace said hello with a businesslike smile. He was in his mid-forties, and everything about him—his wavy hair, mustache, jeans, T-shirt, boots—was black. It wasn't exactly the normal business look that Clay had been expecting.

"Thanks for coming," Max said as they walked into a large, bright, luxuriously-decorated room.

After admiring the view from the window and discussing the economy and sports results for a few minutes, Clay said, "Tell me something about these two firms."

"They don't exist," Max said. "I admit I lied to you, but I promise that I won't lie to you again."

"Who are you?"

"I get hired by big companies to solve difficult problems for them. If they make a big mistake, and realize their mistake before the lawyers do, they hire me to quietly clean up their mess and, hopefully, save them a lot of money. A large company has made a big mistake and I've been hired to help them."

"Which company?"

"I can't tell you my client's name, I'm afraid. If we reach an agreement, I can tell you much more. Here's the story: My client is a multinational company that sells pharmaceuticals. You'll recognize the name. It's an old, well-respected company that makes a wide range of products, from ordinary medicines to complex drugs that will fight cancer and other serious illnesses. About two years ago it produced a drug that might cure serious drug addiction. Let's call this wonder drug Tarvan. It was discovered by mistake and was quickly used on animals in laboratories. The results were amazing, but it wasn't enough to test it only on animals."

"They needed humans," Clay said.

"Yes. Tarvan seemed an important discovery, and the business people in the company were getting very excited. Imagine, if you take one pill a day for ninety days, your addiction to dangerous drugs disappears completely. After that, if you take Tarvan once every *two* days, you're free of the desire for dangerous drugs for life. Almost an immediate cure, for millions of addicts. Think of the profits, think of the lives that would be saved, the crimes that would not be committed, the families that would stay together. The business people wanted Tarvan on the market as soon as possible, but first they had to test it on humans.

"They made a big mistake. They chose three places—Mexico City, Singapore, and Belgrade—and, pretending to be an international aid organization, they built rehab centers, which were really secure places where the addicts could be completely controlled. They chose the worst addicts they could find and began using Tarvan on them."

"Human laboratories," Clay said.

"Far away from the American tort system and the American newspapers. It was an excellent plan, and the drug performed beautifully. After thirty days, Tarvan killed the desire for dangerous drugs. After sixty days, the addicts seemed happy, and after ninety days they had no fear of returning to the streets. Ninety percent stayed on Tarvan, and were cured of the need for dangerous drugs. Only two percent became addicts again."

"And the other eight percent?"

"They became a big problem, but my client didn't know how serious it would be. The company could smell billions of dollars in profit, and there was no competition. Its big mistake was to bring the experiments here. My client wanted to test Tarvan on people in the U.S."

"And?"

"In about eight percent of the patients, something goes wrong. Tarvan makes them killers. After about a hundred days, something happens in their brain and they feel a mysterious but irresistible desire to kill. It makes no difference if they have a violent history or not. Tarvan turns eight percent of the patients into murderers. They stopped using Tarvan in rehab centers here six days ago. The centers in Mexico City, Singapore, and Belgrade were closed down immediately. All experiments have been forgotten. All papers have been destroyed. My client has never heard of Tarvan. We'd like to keep it that way."

"How many murders have there been because of Tarvan here in D.C.?" Clay wanted to know, thinking about Tequila Watson and Washad Porter.

"Five people in D.C. have been killed by addicts on Tarvan— possibly six, if Washad Porter's second victim dies. We know who they are, how they died, who killed them, everything. We want you to represent their families. If you can persuade them to sign their names, we'll pay them money. In this way, things can be dealt with quickly, quietly, with no lawsuits, no publicity, and no more problems for my client."

"Why would the families hire me?"

"Because they don't know that they have a legal case. They think that their loved ones were ordinary victims of street violence. They'll hire you because you'll go to them, tell them that they have a case, and say you can get $4 million in a very quick, secret settlement. Also, you're the only lawyer who is getting close to discovering the truth about Tarvan. If another lawyer finds out about it, there could be a trial. If that happened, my client would lose much more money, and the bad publicity would probably destroy the company. Believe me, Clay, the company knows it's done something bad. It wants to correct it, but it also wants to limit its damages."

"It would be easy to take your client to court and get more money."

"The case would be very hard to prove, Clay, because there's no evidence. The counselors at D Camp and Clean Streets didn't know they were using Tarvan. All the paperwork's been destroyed. The authorities have never heard of Tarvan. And the company would hire the best lawyers in town to defend itself. Litigation would be war because my client is so guilty!"

"Four million dollars for each victim," Clay said thoughtfully. "That's $24 million."

"Add 10 million for the lawyer, Clay. That would be you."

"Ten million? You must be joking."

"We're serious, Clay. A total of $34 million. And I can write the checks immediately."

"I need to go for a walk."

"Would you like some lunch?"

"No thanks."

♦

Clay walked the streets of Washington, D.C., thinking about the offer. One minute, he hated the big pharmaceutical company for doing dangerous experiments on the weakest people it could find. The next minute, he thought about the money. With $10 million, he could marry Rebecca and be free of her family forever. After two hours' thinking about things, he walked into a café and saw Max Pace, sitting alone, drinking lemonade, waiting.

"Did you follow me?"

"Of course. Would you like something to drink?"

"No. What would happen if I represented the Pumphrey family? That case would be worth more than $34 million."

Max seemed ready for the questions. "First, you don't know who to file a lawsuit against. You don't know who made Tarvan. Second, you don't have the money to fight with my client. Third, you'd lose the opportunity to represent all the other known plaintiffs. If you don't say yes quickly, I'll go to the next lawyer on my list with the same offer. I want this whole business finished in thirty days."

"I could go to a big tort firm."

"Yes, but that would give you more problems. First, you'd lose half your fee. Second, the whole business would take five years. Third, there's no guarantee that even the biggest tort firm in the country would win the case. The truth may never be known."

"It should be known."

"Maybe, but I don't care. My job is to silence this thing; to compensate the victims and then forget all about it."

"But I'm defending Tequila Watson. How do I suddenly change sides and represent the victim?"

"As soon as you resign from the OPD, you're free to open your own office and start accepting other cases."

"I don't like that answer."

"It's the best I have. Listen, Clay, Tequila Watson's guilty. Ramón Pumphrey is dead. You have to forget about Watson."

Clay drank his iced water and thought quietly for a minute. He wasn't happy: in his opinion, big corporations should go to jail for crimes the same as ordinary criminals. But if he didn't take the case, another lawyer would …

"OK," he said eventually. "What's your plan?"

Pace pushed his lemonade to one side and leaned forward eagerly. "You leave your job and start your own law firm. Rent a place and put nice furniture in it—you'll need to impress your clients. We've found you a place on Connecticut Avenue. Would you like to see it?"

♦

The office was on the fourth floor of a high, modern glass and metal building on Connecticut Avenue—an expensive, high-class area of Washington, D.C. Expensive carpet was being put down and the walls were being painted.

"The office can be finished in a few days," Pace said as he and Clay stood at a window and watched the traffic below. You can open your new business in less than an hour. Choose a bank, open your accounts … By next Wednesday you can be sitting here behind an expensive desk running your own law firm."

"What about my staff? I'll need other lawyers …"

"Your friends Rodney and Paulette. They know the city and its people. Hire them, pay them three times what they're earning now, and give them nice offices down the hall. They can talk to the families. We'll help."

A short time later, Clay said goodbye to Max and went for another long walk. After that he returned to his office, locked his door, and spent the last hour of the workday thinking about Max Pace's offer, trying to make up his mind.

Later that evening, he met Max Pace for the third time that day. Max talked to him about other work after the Tarvan case finished. "Something much bigger," Max said. He told Clay about another pharmaceutical company which had put a bad drug on the market. "No one knows it yet. Their drug is doing better than my client's drug. But my client now has reliable proof that the bad drug causes cancer. My client has been waiting for the perfect moment to attack. They're planning a class-action lawsuit brought by an aggressive young attorney who possesses the right evidence. After you finish the Tarvan case in thirty days, we'll give you the file on this new case. It will be worth millions. Much more than Tarvan."

Clay looked at Pace with a mixture of surprise and disbelief. "Why me?" he asked quietly.

"You were smart enough to suspect something strange about the Tequila Watson case. Eventually, you might have found out about Tarvan by yourself. We need a bright, young lawyer like you—a man that we can trust. Say yes, and you will become a very big lawyer. Say no, and you'll miss the biggest opportunity of your life."

"I understand, but I still need time to think."

"You have until next Monday."

♦

The next Monday, Clay met Max Pace in a different hotel and sat down to talk business. Pace looked tired, Clay noticed, and more anxious. His smile was gone. The pressure of the Tarvan

25

case was obviously affecting him.

"Washad Porter's second victim died in a hospital last night," Pace said.

"So we have six deaths caused by Tarvan."

"Seven. There was another killing on Saturday morning."

"Are you sure it's a Tarvan case?"

"We're certain."

Clay made a few calculations in his notebook. Then he looked up and said, "I think 5 million for each death caused by Tarvan is a better figure."

"Agreed."

Surprised by Pace's calm acceptance of the new figure, Clay continued, "And I think the attorneys' fees are too low."

"Really?" Pace smiled for the first time. "Ten million isn't enough?"

"No, I'll need at least 15 million."

"That's $50 million altogether?"

"That should be enough."

Pace smiled, and shook Clay's hand. "Agreed," he said. "Congratulations. Now, there's a contract and a few rules for you to follow." Max was reaching into his briefcase.

"What kinds of rules?"

"First, you can never mention Tarvan to Tequila Watson, his new lawyer, or to any of the other criminal defendants involved in this affair. You have to forget about the murderers. You now represent the families of their victims. If you mention Tarvan to anyone, the deal ends and you'll lose everything I'm offering you."

Clay nodded and stared at the thick contract now on the table.

"This is basically a secrecy agreement," Max continued, patting the documents. "It's filled with dark secrets, most of which you won't even be able to tell your secretary. My client's name is never mentioned. Your new clients are getting the money, so they won't be able to ask any questions. We don't think this will be a problem. And we don't expect any moral judgement from you. Just take your money, finish the job, and everybody will be happy."

*Except Tequila Watson*, Clay briefly thought. But soon the only thing that he thought about was the money.

By the end of the day, Clay had signed the paperwork, opened a new bank account, signed a contract for his new offices on Connecticut Avenue, registered as a law firm, resigned from the OPD, persuaded Rodney to join him, and received his first payment from Max Pace—$5 million. He was already a multi-millionaire!

## Chapter 4   Clay's First Clients

Rodney Albritton, Chief Paralegal of the Law Offices of J. Clay Carter, visited Adelfa Pumphrey, who was sitting behind her basement office desk on New York Avenue, staring expressionlessly at the wall of security screens in front of her. Her son had been dead for ten days.

"I'd like to talk to you for a couple of minutes," Rodney said, showing her one of his new business cards.

"About what?" she asked, looking at him with suspicion.

"About your son, Ramón. I know some things about his death that you don't. I'm sorry to be talking about it, but you'll like what I have to say, and I'll be quick."

Adelfa looked at him quietly for a minute. Rodney wasn't like other lawyers she had known; he was smooth, smart, and black, and she wanted to talk to someone.

"Meet me in the café upstairs in twenty minutes," she said.

Twenty minutes later, Rodney was sitting over a coffee, talking to Adelfa. "I work for a lawyer here in town, a young guy, very smart. He's discovered something about your son's

27

death that can get you some big money." Adelfa showed no reaction, so Rodney continued: "The boy that killed Ramón had just walked out of a drug treatment center where he'd been locked up for four months. They'd been giving him some drugs as part of his treatment. We think one of the drugs made him crazy enough to kill your son for no reason."

Adelfa's eyes filled with tears and, for a moment, Rodney thought she was going to cry. But then she looked at him and said, "Big money? How much?"

"More than a million dollars," he said calmly.

"You're joking."

"Why would I do that? I don't know you. There's money on offer, big money. Big corporate drug money that somebody wants you to take and be quiet."

"What big company?"

"Look, I've told you everything I know. My job is to meet you, tell you what's happening, and to invite you to see Mr. Carter, the lawyer I work for."

"A white guy?"

"Yes, and a good guy, too. I've worked with him for five years. You'll like him, and you'll like what he has to say."

"OK," she agreed.

"One important thing," Rodney said, handing her his card and talking almost in a whisper, "This will work only if you keep quiet. It's a big secret. If you do what Mr. Carter advises you to do, you'll get more money than you ever dreamed of. But if people hear about it, you'll get nothing."

♦

Clay had persuaded two more people from the OPD to join him in his new law firm: Miss Glick, the very efficient secretary, and his old friend Paulette Tullos, who was happy to be earning $200,000 a year instead of only $40,000. In addition to these, he had also hired his roommate, Jonah, who had passed his law exam at the fifth attempt but had never practiced law.

After a long discussion with Paulette, Adelfa Pumphrey – the new law firm's very first client – was led down a long hall that smelled of fresh paint to meet Clay, who greeted her warmly and welcomed her into his large new office. His tie was loose, his sleeves were rolled up, and his desk was covered with files and papers, giving the impression that he had many other cases to deal with.

"I recognize you," Adelfa said.

"Yes, I was in court when your son's murderer was formally charged. The judge wanted me to defend him, but I didn't want to. I got rid of the case and now I'm working for the other side. You're probably confused by all this, but it's actually quite simple." He sat on the corner of his desk and told her his version of the big bad drug company. Adelfa listened quietly, not sure what to believe. Clay finished his story by saying, "They want to pay you a lot of money immediately."

"Who, exactly, is *they*?"

"The drug company, but you'll never know its true identity. That's part of the deal. You and I, lawyer and client, must agree to keep everything a secret."

Adelfa thought for a moment, then asked softly, "How much money?"

"Five million dollars."

She covered her eyes and began to cry.

♦

Pace's list of victims stopped at seven. The first on his list (Ramón Pumphrey was sixth) had been a college kid from Bluefield, West Virginia, who had been shot dead as he was walking out of a Starbucks coffee shop. Clay made the five-hour journey there in his brand new black Porsche Carrera, and parked in front of a small, sad-looking one-floor house.

The dead student's mother let him in and offered him tea and cookies. Clay sat on a sofa in a room with pictures of the dead son everywhere and waited for the father, an insurance salesman, to arrive home. He then presented his case to them, as much of it as possible. They asked him several questions—How many others died because of this drug? Why can't we go to the authorities? Shouldn't we tell the newspapers?—but Clay was ready for them all.

"If you can't tell me the real name of the company, then I won't accept the money," the father said at one point.

"I don't *know* the real name," Clay replied.

Like all victims, they had a choice. They could get angry, ask questions, demand justice, or they could quietly take the money. The parents were very confused; during the afternoon and into the evening, they experienced all kinds of emotions but, just after 10 P.M., Clay finally persuaded them to sign the paperwork.

♦

The last Tarvan clients to sign the documents were the parents of a twenty-year-old student who had left university and had been murdered one week later. They sat in Clay's office for an hour, holding hands tightly, crying as they talked about their daughter. Eventually they signed the paperwork, and Paulette and Miss Glick accompanied them out of the office and to the elevators where, after a tearful goodbye, the doors closed.

Clay's little team met in the conference room and talked quietly for a moment, grateful that there were no more widows and grief-filled parents to interview. Some very expensive drink had been iced for the occasion, and Clay began pouring. During the second bottle, Clay rose to speak.

"I have some announcements," he said, tapping his glass. "First, the Tylenol cases are now complete. Congratulations and thanks to you all." He had used Tylenol as a code for Tarvan, a name they would never hear. Nor would they ever know the amount of his fees. Obviously, Clay was being paid a lot of money, but they had no idea how much. "Second, we begin the celebration tonight with dinner at Citronelle." Everybody laughed and cheered. "Third, in two weeks, we leave for seven days in Paris, first-class flights, luxury hotel, all expenses paid."

There was more wild cheering and laughter. Seven nights in Paris! No one could believe it. A month earlier, they had all been working long hours for little money at the OPD—apart from Jonah, who had been selling computers part-time.


## Chapter 5    Dyloft


The next day, Max Pace visited Clay in the office, which was closed for the day after the previous night's long celebrations.

"You did good work, Clay," he said. "I'll transfer the rest of the money into your bank today. You're doing a great job of looking rich. But be careful. Don't create too much attention."

"Let's talk about the next case."

Pace sat down. "The drug is Dyloft, manufactured by Ackerman Labs★. It's used by sufferers of severe arthritis. It's a new drug. It works very well, and patients love it. But it has two problems: first, it's made by a competitor of my client; second, it's been linked to the creation of small tumors in the bladder. My client, the same client as Tarvan, makes a similar drug that was popular until twelve months ago, when Dyloft became available. Dyloft is growing fast; it's already number two in the market, and will soon be number one. A few months ago, my

★ Labs: the short form of *Laboratories*

31

client discovered documents that prove that Ackerman Labs has known about the possible problems with Dyloft for six months. Are you following me?"

"Yes. How many people have taken Dyloft?"

"Probably a million."

"What percentage get the tumors?"

"About five percent."

"You want me to sue Ackerman Labs?"

"The truth about Dyloft will be public knowledge very soon. There hasn't been any litigation yet, but Ackerman is getting ready. It's busy counting its money and saving it to pay the lawyers. The company has a real problem because it's borrowed too much, and now it needs cash. The value of the company is already falling, and the news about Dyloft will probably destroy it completely, which is exactly what my client wants. From inside the company we have proof that Dyloft is bad, and it will have to settle. It will have no choice. But there's one small problem for us in all this. Most of the tumors don't seem to be dangerous, and they're very small. There's no real damage to the bladder."

"So the litigation will be used to shock the market?"

"Yes—and, of course, to compensate the victims. Here's my plan: you put together a group of fifty plaintiffs and file a big lawsuit on behalf of all Dyloft patients. At the same time you put out a series of TV advertisements soliciting more cases. If you move quickly, you'll get thousands of cases. People will be scared and will phone your free number here in D.C., where you'll have at least half a dozen paralegals answering the calls. It will cost you a lot of money but if you get, for example, five thousand cases at $20,000 each, that's $100 million—and your share is one third."

"That's terrible!"

"No, Clay, that's mass tort litigation at its finest. That's how the system works." Pace slid a thick file across Clay's desk. "There are the names and addresses of at least a thousand possible plaintiffs in here. I also have the name of a company that can prepare a television advertisement which will bring you thousands of extra clients. The whole thing will cost you a couple of million dollars, but you can afford it. First, you get the clients to sign contracts with your firm, which will take about two weeks. It will take three days to finish the TV advertisement, and a few days to buy the television time. You'll need to hire paralegals and put them in a rented space out in the suburbs; it's too expensive here. The lawsuit has to be prepared. You have a good staff. Everything should be done in about thirty days. My client wants the lawsuit filed in less than a month."

Clay stood up and walked anxiously around the room. He didn't like the idea of soliciting clients with TV advertisements—it was unprofessional. In addition, he had never handled a lawsuit like this before. But $33 million in fees! He couldn't possibly refuse!

♦

"We have work to do," Clay began the meeting in the conference room. He told Paulette, Rodney, and Jonah about Dyloft and its disastrous side effects. "Nobody's filed a lawsuit yet, but we're going to change that. On July 2nd, we start the war by filing a class action here in D.C. on behalf of all the patients harmed by the drug. We have some names and addresses and we start signing up those clients today. Paulette and Rodney, you'll be in charge of that. Jonah, you'll be in charge of employing half a dozen paralegals and finding space out in the suburbs for them to take calls from possible new clients."

"How much is each Dyloft case worth?" Paulette asked.

"As much as Ackerman Labs will pay. It could be anything from $10,000 to $50,000, depending on the extent of damage to the bladder."

"And how many cases might we get?"

"After the series of advertisements we'll be putting on TV, it could be several thousand."

"And how much are the attorneys' fees?" Paulette asked. The other two were watching Clay very carefully.

"One third," he said.

"So if we have three thousand clients, for example, the firm will get $10 million?"

"Yes. And we're going to share the fees. Ten percent to each of you."

"So, that could mean $1 million each?"

"At least," Clay replied.

They thought about that figure in silence for a very long time, each one imagining how they would be spending the money. For Rodney, it meant college for the kids. For Paulette, it meant a divorce from the Greek husband she had only seen once in the past year. For Jonah, it meant life on a sailboat.

Clay was the first to break the silence. "If we work really hard for the next year, there's a good chance we'll have the option of early retirement."

"Who told you about Dyloft?" Rodney wanted to know.

"I can never answer that question, Rodney. Sorry. Just trust me."

And at that moment, Clay hoped that his blind trust in Max Pace wasn't foolish.

♦

On the third floor of his new town house, Clay made his first entry into the world of mass tort solicitation. He delayed the call until almost 9 P.M., an hour when some people went to bed, especially older people, and maybe those suffering with arthritis. After a strong drink to give him courage, he dialed a number.

The phone was answered on the other end by Mrs. Ted

Worley of Upper Marlboro, Maryland. Clay introduced himself pleasantly as a lawyer and asked to speak to Mr. Worley. Clay heard some voices in the background, the sound of a baseball game on TV, then finally a man's voice on the phone.

"Who is this?" Ted Worley angrily demanded. "I don't like being interrupted when I'm watching baseball."

"I'm an attorney here in D.C., and I specialize in lawsuits against companies that manufacture harmful drugs."

"OK, what do you want?"

"We found your name on the Internet as a possible user of the arthritis drug Dyloft. Can you tell me if you use this drug?"

"Maybe I don't want to tell you."

"Of course you don't have to, Mr. Worley. But the only way to discover if you're entitled to a settlement is to tell me if you're using the drug."

"What kind of settlement?"

"We'll talk about that in a minute. First, I need to know if you're using Dyloft. If not, you're a lucky man."

"Yeah, I've been taking Dyloft."

"For how long?"

"Maybe a year. It works great."

"Any side effects such as blood in your urine, a burning sensation when you urinate?"

"No. Why?"

"The drug has been found to cause bladder tumors in some people who use it. Ackerman Labs, the company that makes Dyloft, has been trying to keep this secret. My firm represents a lot of Dyloft users. I think you should consider being tested."

"What kind of test?"

"A urine test. We have a doctor who can do it tomorrow. It won't cost you anything."

"What if he finds something wrong?"

"Then we can discuss your options. When the news of Dyloft

comes out in a few days' time, there will be many lawsuits. My firm will lead the attack on Ackerman Labs. I'd like to have you as a client."

"Should I stop taking the drug?"

"Let's do the test first. Dyloft will probably be pulled off the market later this summer."

"Where do I do the test?"

Clay gave him the name and address of a doctor that Max Pace had chosen for him. When the details were finished, Clay apologized for interrupting the baseball game and said goodbye. It was only then that he realized that his forehead was covered in sweat. *Soliciting clients by phone? What kind of lawyer have I become? A rich one*, he kept telling himself.

♦

Two days later, Clay visited Ted Worley. The urine test had revealed unusual cells in the urine, a clear sign that there were tumors in the bladder. Although the operation to remove them would not be complicated, Ted Worley and his wife were extremely worried. Clay wanted to tell them that the tumors weren't dangerous, but decided to let the doctor tell them that after the operation. After Clay had explained the contract and answered their questions about litigation, Ted Worley signed the papers and became the first Dyloft plaintiff in the country.

By the end of the week, Clay had signed up three clients with unusual cells in their urine. Rodney and Paulette, working as a team, had seven more under contract. The Dyloft class action was ready for war.

♦

On July 1st, everyone gathered in front of the television in the conference room to watch the fifteen-second advertisement advising Dyloft users to call the firm and arrange a free medical

36

test. Two hours later, all six paralegals employed for this job were busy answering calls.

At nine the next morning, Clay received an urgent phone call from the Ackerman Labs' attorney. He ordered Clay to stop running the advertisements immediately. The conversation was short and angry, and when it was ended Clay sent Rodney to the attorney's office with a copy of the twenty-page lawsuit against Ackerman Labs.

Later that day, Max Pace visited Clay.

"I've filed the lawsuit," Clay told him. "We've created a lot of excitement. Their lawyers have already called, and I sent them a copy of the lawsuit."

"Good. They know they're in big trouble. This is a lawyer's dream, Clay. Enjoy the moment."

"If you were Ackerman's lawyer," Clay asked, "what would you do next?"

"I'd deny everything, blame it on the greedy trial lawyers. Defend my drug. My first aim would be to protect the price of shares in the company. I'd get the Chief Executive Officer on television to say all the right things. I'd get the lawyers to prepare an organized defense. I'd get the sales people to persuade the doctors that the drug is OK. Then I'd have a serious talk with Ackerman Labs. If I found out there were real problems with the drug, I'd calculate how much a settlement would cost. You never go to trial with a bad drug, because you can't control the costs. So if I were Ackerman's lawyer, I'd settle for about a billion dollars—and I'd do it fast."

"Will Ackerman do it fast?"

"They haven't hired me, so they're not very bright. They prefer to do it the old-fashioned way—they rely on lawyers, who, of course, have no interest in quick settlements."

"So no quick settlement?"

"You filed the lawsuit less than an hour ago. Relax."

"I know, but all that money you just gave me is going very quickly."

"Relax. In a year's time, you'll be even richer."

♦

The following morning, the *Times* and the *Post* printed brief stories of the Dyloft class action on the front pages of their business sections. Both mentioned Clay's name. Both noted that the price of Ackerman Labs' shares was falling fast. A photograph of Clay and his team appeared in the *Wall Street Journal*. In the same newspaper, under the headline: YOUNG LAWYER FIGHTS POWERFUL ACKERMAN LABS, there was an article about Clay and his amazing rise to the top as an important, successful tort lawyer. Clay gave a copy of the article to Jonah.

"Put this on the Internet," he said. "Our clients will love it."

## Chapter 6   The Lawsuit Against Ackerman Labs

Tequila Watson pleaded guilty to the murder of Ramón Pumphrey and was given life imprisonment. Clay saw the story and felt a little guilty. He owed something to Tequila, but he wasn't sure what. There was no way of compensating his former client. He tried to tell himself that Tequila would probably have spent the rest of his life in prison anyway, with or without Tarvan, but this didn't make Clay feel any better. The truth was, he had taken the cash and buried the truth.

At that moment, Miss Glick rang his office with a message that soon made Clay forget his guilty feelings over Tequila Watson: Patton French, the most successful tort lawyer in the country, wanted to talk to him!

Later that day, Clay was on board Patton French's private jet at Reagan National Airport. Clay was extremely impressed—the inside of the jet was more like a five-star hotel. French shook Clay's hand and invited him to sit as the plane took off for New York.

"I was thinking about suing Ackerman two months ago," French informed him, "but you did it first. However, I think we can do business together. There's a lot of money out there." Then, noticing Clay's undisguised admiration for the inside of the plane, he said, "Do you have a jet yet?"

"No," Clay replied, feeling suddenly inadequate.

"It won't be long, son. A top lawyer can't live without his own jet."

After congratulating Clay again on his lawsuit against Dyloft, French made him an offer:

"Soon, I'll have as many Dyloft cases as you. Now that you've opened the door, there will be hundreds of lawyers chasing these cases. You and I can control the litigation if we move your lawsuit from D.C. to my home territory in Mississippi. If we join your cases with mine in one enormous class action, Ackerman Labs will be frightened beyond all imagination."

Clay's head was spinning with doubts and questions. "I'm listening," he said quietly.

"You keep your cases, I'll keep mine. As more cases come in, we'll form a Plaintiffs' Guidance Committee. I'll be the chairman. You'll be on the committee because you filed your lawsuit first. We'll keep the Dyloft litigation organized. I've done it dozens of times. The committee gives us control. We'll start discussing things with Ackerman very soon. I know their lawyers. If your inside information is as strong as you say, we'll push hard for an early settlement."

"How early?"

"That depends on several things. How many cases are really out there? How quickly can we sign them up? How many other lawyers file lawsuits? And, very important, how severe is the damage to our clients?"

"Not very severe. Very few of the tumors are dangerous."

French thought for a moment, then said, "That's good. It's better for our clients, because they're not as sick as they could be, and better for us because the settlements will come faster. The important thing is for us to get as many cases as we can. The more cases we get, the more control we have over the class action. More cases, more fees."

"I understand," Clay said.

After further discussions with French in New York about the financial details of the lawsuit (French was going to provide another million dollars for medical tests; Clay was going to double his spending on advertising; both agreed that they would take forty percent of the final settlement, plus expenses), Clay telephoned Max Pace for his advice. Max was enthusiastic. "Do it!" he said. "And read the *New York Times* tomorrow morning. There's a big story about Dyloft. The first medical report has been published. Ackerman Labs won't be happy at all!"

Clay met French for dinner in a top Manhattan restaurant, signed the contract that French had prepared, and agreed to let French file the class action against Ackerman Labs in Biloxi, Mississippi, the next day.

♦

The next morning, Clay got up early and read the news of the first medical reports on Dyloft: bladder tumors had been found in six percent of those who had used Dyloft for more than a year. Some doctors had already decided to stop using the drug. Ackerman Labs offered a weak denial, blaming greedy trial lawyers for exaggerating the news. Ackerman's shares had fallen to $32.50.

By the time Clay returned to his office later that day, Ackerman shares were at $28. The first person he met in his office was Jonah.

"We were here until midnight last night," Jonah said. "It's crazy."

"It's going to get crazier," Clay replied. "We're doubling the TV ads. Hire some more paralegals."

Jonah started to leave, but stopped at the door.

"What is it?" Clay asked.

"Do you know what you're doing? You're spending money faster than anyone can count it. What if something goes wrong?"

"Are you worried?"

"We're all a little worried, OK?"

"I'll be honest with you," Clay said, sitting on the corner of his desk. "We're taking a huge gamble, and I've never done this kind of thing before. If we win, we make a lot of money. If we lose, we're still in business. We won't be rich, that's all."

Patton French called late in the afternoon and reported that the class action against Ackerman Labs, which had been changed to include his Mississippi plaintiffs, had been filed in a state court in Biloxi.

"I'll close the lawsuit here tomorrow," Clay said, hoping that he was doing the right thing.

Ackerman Labs shares fell to $26.25. Clay, who, on Max Pace's advice, had sold his own Ackerman shares a few days earlier, before they had started to fall, would make a profit of $1,625,000 if he bought them back now. But he decided to wait. After news of the Biloxi lawsuit reached the papers, Ackerman shares would be even cheaper.

♦

As more medical studies about Dyloft were published, the Government Drugs Agency finally ordered that the drug should be taken off the market. The threat of tumors had persuaded almost all Dyloft users to contact a lawyer. Patton French had never seen a mass tort class action come together so beautifully.

41

He succeeded in persuading other lawyers who were filing lawsuits against Ackerman Labs to join his lawsuit in Biloxi. In mid-August, French chaired a meeting of the Dyloft Plaintiffs' Guidance Committee at his enormous ranch in Idaho. There, Clay met some of the richest lawyers in America, and they were all eager to meet him. They wanted to know how he had discovered the Dyloft case, but he refused to tell them. French told everybody that he had had private meetings with Ackerman Labs' lawyers, and they had told him that Ackerman wanted to settle quickly, otherwise the company wouldn't survive. All French's talk centered on how much money Ackerman were willing to pay and how much all the lawyers would receive; he said nothing, Clay noticed, about the clients. In sixty days' time, there would be a settlement conference with Ackerman Labs. Dyloft looked as if it would be the quickest settlement in mass tort history, and the lawyers could already smell the money.

♦

Clay's firm had hired two more lawyers and now had ten paralegals, none of whom had more than three months' experience, except for Rodney. There were 3,320 new Dyloft cases, each of which needed immediate attention.

"They want someone to talk to," Jonah complained, "and we don't have enough people to talk to them. I'm afraid we'll be losing clients very soon."

"How many more staff do we need?" Clay asked.

"At least ten," Jonah said. "Maybe more later. And we also need to hire a doctor for a year, someone to organize the tests and medical evidence."

"And we need one full-time person producing and mailing a newsletter to clients who don't use the Internet," Paulette added.

"Get it done," Clay agreed.

Paulette looked at Jonah with a worried look. Jonah put down his notebook and looked at Clay.

"Clay, we're spending huge amounts of money," he said. "Are you sure you know what you're doing?"

"No, but I think so. Just trust me, OK? We're all going to make some serious money. But to do that, we have to spend some cash."

"And you have the cash?" asked Paulette, who, like the others, knew nothing about the details of Clay's arrangement with Patton French.

"We do," Clay assured her.

♦

Max Pace wanted a late drink with Clay in a bar in Georgetown, not far from Clay's town house. Halfway through the first beer, Pace started talking about Dyloft, and advised Clay to buy back the shares in Ackerman Labs that he had sold a few days earlier. "Buy back as many shares as you can," he said, "and wait for their value to double."

At 10 A.M. the next morning, Clay bought back his Ackerman shares at $23, making a profit of $1.9 million. With this profit, he bought another two hundred thousand shares. He watched the market on the Internet all morning, but there was no movement in the price of the shares.

At 5 P.M., a company called Philo Products announced that it would buy the rest of Ackerman shares. As he watched the news alone on the big screen in his conference room, Clay had many questions he wanted to ask: Was Philo Pace's secret client? Was it the company that had made Tarvan? Were the Dyloft cases just an excuse to weaken Ackerman Labs so that Philo could buy it at a low price? What would happen to Ackerman Labs and the case against Dyloft now?

Patton French told Clay on the phone not to worry. "This

43

is good news. If Philo buys Ackerman Labs, they'll settle the Dyloft cases quickly and quietly. Philo hates going to court."

*That sounds like Tarvan*, Clay thought.

♦

Rex Crittle, Clay's accountant, was worried. "Your firm is six months old," he said, looking up from a pile of reports on his desk, "but you're already spending half a million dollars a month!"

"You have to spend it to make it," Clay said, calmly drinking his coffee and enjoying his accountant's discomfort.

"But no money has come in for three months," Crittle complained.

"It's been a good year."

"Oh yes. $15 million in fees makes a wonderful year. But the money's going fast. You used $14,000 last month on private jet travel."

"That reminds me," Clay said. "I'm thinking of buying a jet."

"You can't afford one."

"We'll soon have more money."

"I assume you're talking about the Dyloft cases? $4 million for advertising, $3,000 a month each for the Dyloft Internet site and newsletter, all these new paralegals and lawyers …"

"I'd prefer a Gulfstream." Clay wasn't interested in Crittle's anxieties. "It's the finest jet in the world. It would cost about $45 million."

"You don't have $45 million!"

"You're right. But maybe I'll rent one …"

Crittle shook his head with a sigh of disapproval. "It's your money, I guess."

♦

The meeting between the Dyloft Plaintiffs' Guidance Committee and Ackerman Labs took place in New York City, in the dance hall of an old hotel near Central Park. One week earlier, the government had approved of Philo Products' purchase of Ackerman (which meant that Clay had made another profit of $6 million). Patton French did most of the talking: the Biloxi class-action lawsuit had 36,700 plaintiffs. A group of lawyers in Georgia had another 5,200 clients and were threatening another class action, but French wasn't worried about them because they didn't have the important documents that *he* had. Clay listened, but was bored by all the figures. The only number that interested him was 5,380, which was his share of the Dyloft cases. He still had more than any single lawyer, although French himself was close, with just over 5,000.

After three hours of non-stop figures, everyone agreed on a one-hour lunch break. After a couple of sandwiches and a glass of water, Clay went for a walk up Fifth Avenue, accompanied by Wes Saulsberry, another member of the Guidance Committee.

"I've found out about another little mass tort that you might be interested in," Saulsberry informed him. "I'm too busy."

"I'm listening," Clay replied.

"The company is in Reedsburg, Pennsylvania, and it makes the cement used by bricklayers in new home construction. It seems they're having problems with their cement. After about three years, it begins to break down, and when it does, the bricks start falling. It affects about two thousand homes in the Baltimore area, and it's just beginning to get noticed."

"What are the damages?"

"It costs about $15,000 to fix each house."

Thirty-three percent of $15,000 multiplied by two thousand equaled $10 million. Clay was getting quick with his figures.

"The proof will be easy," Saulsberry said. "The company knows it's made a mistake. Settlement shouldn't be a problem."

"I'd like to look at it."

"I'll send you the file, but don't tell anyone I told you."

"Why are you telling me about it?"

"It's my way of saying thank you for Dyloft. Of course, if you get the chance to return the favor some day, then it will be appreciated. That's how we tort lawyers work, Clay. We're all greedy and competitive, but a few of us try to help each other."

♦

Late in the afternoon, Ackerman Labs agreed to a minimum of $62,000 for each of the forty thousand Dyloft plaintiffs, and the money would be available immediately.

"Not a bad day's work," French smiled at the end of the meeting, handing Clay a printed summary of his cases and anticipated fees: $106 million.

As soon as he was alone, Clay called Paulette at his office in D.C. "You've just made $10 million," he told her.

After talking to Jonah and Rodney, he sat on his bed for a long time, sad with the realization that he had no one else to talk to. He thought of Rebecca, and decided to call her. She answered the phone after three rings.

"It's Clay," he said, trying to sound casual.

"Hello, stranger," she said politely.

"How are you?"

"Fine, busy as always. I hear things are going well for you."

"I can't complain. How's your job?"

"I'm finishing in six more days. I'm getting married, you know."

"Yes, I heard. When's the wedding?"

"December 20th."

"I haven't received an invitation."

"I didn't send you one. I didn't think you'd want to come."

"Probably not. Are you sure you want to get married?"

"Let's talk about something else."

"Don't do it, Rebecca. Don't marry him …"

The line went dead.

Clay stretched out on the bed and stared at the ceiling, still hearing Rebecca's voice, hit hard with the realization of how much he still missed her.

◆

When Ted Worley received a thick envelope from the Law Offices of J. Clay Carter, he immediately opened it. He had seen various news reports about the Dyloft settlement, and had been waiting to collect his money from Ackerman Labs.

The letter began, "Dear Mr. Worley: Congratulations. Your class-action claim against Ackerman Labs has been settled in the U.S. District Court for the Southern District of Mississippi. Your portion of the settlement is $62,000. According to the contract signed by you with this firm, twenty-eight percent of this settlement will go on attorneys' fees. In addition, $1,400 will go on litigation expenses, approved by the court. You will therefore receive, as a final settlement, a total of $43,240. Please sign the enclosed agreement and return it immediately in the enclosed envelope."

$43,240! Was that all he would receive from that criminal pharmaceutical company that deliberately sold a drug that had caused four tumors to grow in his bladder? $43,240 for months of fear and anxiety about living or dying? $43,240 for the painful surgery to remove the four tumors, and three days of lumps and blood in his urine?

He called Clay's law firm six times and left six angry messages on the answer machine. Finally, one of Clay's lawyers called him back.

"This settlement is a joke!" Mr. Worley said. "Forty-three thousand dollars is criminal."

"Your settlement is sixty-two thousand, Mr. Worley," the young attorney said.

"I'm getting forty-three."

"No, you're getting sixty-two. You agreed to give one third to your attorney, without whom you would be getting nothing. That figure has been reduced to twenty-eight percent by the settlement. Most lawyers charge forty-five or fifty percent."

"Well, I'm not accepting it!"

"If the settlements were bigger, Ackerman Labs would go bankrupt and that would leave you with even less."

"I'm still not accepting the settlement."

"You have no choice. Look at the Contract for Legal Services, Mr. Worley, page eleven, paragraph eight. You'll see that you gave this firm authority to settle for anything above $50,000."

"I remember that, but I was told that that was a starting point. I was expecting much more."

"Your settlement has already been approved by the court, sir. That's the way class actions work. If you don't sign the acceptance form, your portion will eventually go to someone else."

"You're a lot of criminals, you know that? I don't know who's worse—the company that made the drug or the lawyers who are robbing me of a fair settlement."

"I'm sorry you feel that way."

"You're not sorry about anything. The newspaper says you're getting $100 million. Thieves!"

Mr. Worley put down the phone angrily and threw the papers across his kitchen.


## Chapter 7   The Wedding Party

The December cover of *Capitol Magazine* featured Clay Carter, looking rich and handsome in his expensive Armani suit. Inside there were pictures of him playing with a dog (borrowed from Rodney), standing proudly in empty courtrooms, washing his new Porsche, and standing on board his new boat in the

Bahamas. Near the back of the same magazine were pictures of brides, followed by announcements of future weddings. There was a picture of Rebecca Van Horn, looking beautiful, sitting on a bench next to her future husband, an insignificant but rich-looking man called Jason Schubert Myers. Clay smiled to himself at the misery the magazine must, at that moment, be causing in the Van Horn home. Bennett and Barbara Van Horn wanted the whole world to be impressed by their daughter's wedding, but who was on the front cover of the same magazine? Clay Carter, the man who Bennett had called a loser. Revenge was sweet. But his revenge wasn't finished yet.

"I'm looking for a young woman, preferably a blonde," Clay said to Jonah after work that Wednesday evening.

Jonah was surprised. "The richest young bachelor in town is having trouble finding a woman?"

"I'm going to Rebecca's wedding, and I need a beautiful young woman to go with me."

Jonah knew hundreds of beautiful women, and he showed Clay a photograph in a magazine of a girl called Ridley—a twenty-five-year-old fashion model from Russia who had come to America as a student and who had never gone back.

Clay met Ridley for dinner in a Japanese restaurant, and was amazed to see that she looked even more beautiful in person than she did in her photographs. Conversation wasn't easy—she spoke five languages, but her English was poor—but Clay didn't mind. *Dinner now, Rebecca's wedding later, then it's thank you and goodbye*, Clay thought.

♦

On the day of Rebecca's wedding, as he turned into the drive of the Potomac Country Club, Clay remembered his last visit to the same place, seven months earlier. Then he had hidden his old Honda behind the tennis courts, but now he was proudly driving a brand new Porsche.

They were an hour late, which was perfect timing. The dance hall was crowded and a jazz band played at one end. Heads began turning immediately as Ridley entered the room, and many men who, in normal circumstances, would have ignored Clay, suddenly wanted to shake his hand. Ridley squeezed Clay's arm tightly as a crowd of Clay's old "friends" pressed in on all sides, wanting to say hello, laughing at everything Clay said as if he were the funniest man in the world, but all the time looking at Ridley.

An announcement was being made onstage and the room became quieter. The bride and groom were going to dance, and the crowd gathered round to watch. Rebecca looked very beautiful as she slowly danced with her husband around the dance floor, and Clay felt jealous and angry.

"You still love her, don't you?" Ridley whispered.

"Not now," he whispered back.

"You do. I can tell."

"No."

It was painful to watch Rebecca dancing with her husband, and Clay had to remind himself why he was there: he wanted Rebecca to see him with a beautiful girl, and to know that he was doing very well without her. He took Ridley by the hand and led her to the dance floor, where a lot of other people were now already dancing. Ridley was a natural dancer, and groups of men soon gathered round to watch her carefully. Rebecca, too, noticed her, and then saw, to her surprise, that this beautiful, sexy, blonde woman was dancing with Clay! The music ended and, just as a slow song was beginning, Rebecca stepped between Clay and Ridley.

"Hello, Clay," she said, ignoring Ridley. "How about a dance?"

"Sure," he said.

Ridley moved away, but she wasn't alone for long. Within seconds, she was surrounded by dozens of men. She chose the tallest one, threw her arms around him, and began to dance.

"I don't remember inviting you," Rebecca said with an arm over Clay's shoulder.

"Do you want me to leave?" he said, pulling her as close to him as her wedding dress would allow.

"People are watching," she said, smiling for their benefit. "Why are you here?"

"To celebrate your wedding and to see your lovely new husband."

"Don't be unpleasant, Clay. You're just jealous."

"I'm more than jealous. I'd like to break his neck."

"Jason's not bad."

"I don't want to hear about it. Just promise me you won't get pregnant, OK?"

"That's not your business."

"Tell me that you still love me."

"I don't."

"You're lying."

"It might be best if you left now." Rebecca pulled away from him. Then, looking at Ridley dancing, added, "And take her with you."

"Just wait a year, OK?" Clay ignored her request. "By then, I'll have $200 million. We can jump on my jet, leave this boring little place and spend the rest of our lives on my boat. Your parents will never find us."

She stood in front of him, not moving, and said, "Goodbye, Clay."

"I'll wait," he said, then got knocked to one side by Bennett, who grabbed his daughter, and rescued her by leading her to the other side of the floor.

Barbara was next. She took Clay's hand and flashed him an artificial smile. "Don't cause any trouble, Clay," she said without moving her lips. She pretended to dance with him, leading him

51

toward the door.

"And how are you, Mrs. Van Horn?" Clay said, his politeness as artificial as her smile.

"Fine, until I saw you. I'm sure you weren't invited to this party."

"I was just leaving."

"Good. I'd hate to call security."

"That won't be necessary."

The music stopped and Clay pulled away from Mrs. Van Horn, marched across the dance floor, pulled Ridley away from her crowd of admiring men and led her toward the bar. As he was ordering a drink, a big man in a rented suit approached him and whispered, "I'm security."

"I'm leaving," Clay whispered in reply.

Driving away from the great Potomac Country Club, with Ridley wrapped around him, Clay privately told himself that this was one of the finest moments of his life.

## Chapter 8    Maxatil

Clay, Jonah, Paulette, and Rodney were spending less and less time at the office, trying to avoid the angry phone calls from Dyloft clients who were unhappy with their small settlements. Several clients had actually come to the office in person, demanding to see Clay, but Miss Glick always told them that he was away on business. Usually, Clay was hiding in his office with the door locked. After one particularly bad day, he called Patton French for advice.

"Be brave," French told him. "It's all part of the job. You're making a fortune in mass torts, but this is the negative side."

♦

Clay took Ridley to spend Christmas with him in his new house on the Caribbean island of Mustique. Two days after Christmas, Max Pace arrived, wanting to talk business.

"There's another drug out there," Pace said, "and it's a big one. But the plan is a little different this time. I want a share of the profits."

"Who are you working for?"

"Me. And you. I want twenty-five percent of the attorneys' fees. This could be bigger than Dyloft."

"Agreed," Clay said without hesitation and shook Pace's hand. "Now give me the details."

"There's a female hormone drug called Maxatil. It's used by at least 4 million women aged between forty-five and seventy-five. It came out five years ago, and it gives them relief from discomfort caused by menopause. It's very effective, and is supposed to preserve bone strength. The company is Goffman."

"Goffman? Razor blades and mouthwash?"

"That's right. Twenty-one billion dollars in sales last year, very little debt, good management—a perfect example of a successful American company. But they were in too much of a hurry with Maxatil. The typical story—the profits looked huge, the drug looked safe. They managed to get quick approval from the Government Drugs Agency and for the first few years everybody was happy. Doctors loved it, and women are crazy about it because it works so beautifully."

"But?"

"But there are problems. Huge problems. A government study has been looking carefully at twenty thousand of these women. Its report will be published in a few weeks, and the news for these women and for Goffman is not good. For about eight percent of the women, the drug greatly increases the risk of breast cancer and heart disease. Very few people know about the report, but I have a copy of it. One lawsuit has already been

53

filed in Flagstaff, Arizona, but it's not a class action. It's just an old-fashioned individual tort case."

"How boring."

"Not really. The lawyer is a man named Dale Mooneyham, from Tucson. He tries his cases one at a time and he never loses. His case against Goffman will go to trial before any other lawsuits can be filed. If he succeeds, then the way is clear for you to make a fortune with a class action against the same company. The important thing is to file your class action first. You learned that from Patton French."

"We can file first," Clay said.

"And you can do it alone, without French. File it in D.C., then put a lot of ads out on TV. It'll be huge."

"Just like Dyloft."

"Except this time you're in charge. I'll be helping in the background, doing the dirty work. I know a lot of important people. It'll be our lawsuit, and with your name on it Goffman will be very frightened."

"A quick settlement?"

"Probably not as quick as Dyloft, but that was unusually fast. You'll have to push hard for the first trial, persuade Goffman that you're not interested in a settlement, that you want a trial—a huge, public trial. There are no hidden problems, although it will cost you millions in advertising and preparations for the trial. And I'd like an advance payment of a million dollars."

Clay was puzzled by Pace's request for money. However, with the chance of another big money-making tort case and their shared Tarvan secret, he couldn't say no.

♦

January was a very busy month for Clay. Jonah and Paulette finally left the firm (Jonah wanted to spend his life sailing on his new boat, Paulette had gone to London for a vacation and emailed Clay to say that she didn't want to work any more), but Clay was busy hiring plenty of new staff to replace them. Soon after Christmas, he assigned three lawyers, two paralegals and three secretaries to the Maxatil litigation. He also assigned two lawyers and a paralegal to prepare a class action against the company in Reedsburg, Pennsylvania, that was making poor quality cement. He was invited to an official state dinner honoring the President of Argentina at the White House, where he and Ridley had their picture taken with the President of the United States. And, to the horror of Rex Crittle, he bought a snow-white private jet, a Gulfstream, for $30 million.

Goffman, meanwhile, was enjoying excellent sales. Profits were up, and the price of its shares was $65, the highest for two years. At the beginning of January, it had started an unusual series of advertisements promoting not just its products but the company itself. "Goffman has always been there," the advertisements proudly announced. All their previous advertising had been about one particular product, and Clay was sure that these new advertisements were Goffman's way of preparing its investors and customers for the shock of Maxatil. His opinion was shared by Max Pace, who was now staying at the Hay-Adams Hotel. He seemed anxious when Clay visited for a late dinner, impatient for the class action against Goffman to begin.

"What's the plan?" Pace wanted to know, ignoring the food and wine.

Clay wasn't ignoring his. "The ads start at eight in the morning—coast to coast. The telephone lines and Internet site are ready. I'll walk over to the courthouse at about ten o'clock and file the lawsuit myself."

"Sounds good."

"We've done it before. The Law Offices of J. Clay Carter are now an experienced tort machine."

"You haven't told Patton French or the other lawyers, have you?"

T042074

"Of course not. Why would I tell them? We helped each other over Dyloft, but those guys are my competitors, too. I've shocked them before, I'll shock them again. I can't wait."

"This isn't Dyloft—remember that. You were lucky before because you caught a weak company at a bad moment. Goffman will be much tougher."

"But they made a bad drug," Clay replied, "and you don't go to trial with a bad drug."

"Not in a class action. My sources tell me that Goffman might want to litigate the case in Flagstaff since that's a single plaintiff."

"The Mooneyham case?"

"That's it. If they lose, they'll want to reach an early settlement. But if they win, this could be a long fight."

"You said Mooneyham never loses."

"He hasn't lost for twenty years. Juries love him. He wears cowboy hats and red boots—old-fashioned maybe, but a real character. You should go and meet him. You'd learn a lot."

"I'll put that on my list," Clay replied, excited about using his new Gulfstream jet.

♦

At eight o'clock the next morning, everybody crowded into the conference room and stared at the wide-screen TV, waiting for the first ad to appear:

An attractive woman in her early sixties was sitting at a small kitchen table, staring sadly out of a window. A voice said, "If you've been taking the female hormone drug Maxatil, you may have an increased risk of breast cancer or heart disease." The camera moved in on the woman's hands; on the table next to them was a bottle with the word MAXATIL on the label. The voice continued: "Please consult your doctor immediately. Maxatil may seriously threaten your health." The camera showed a close-up of the woman's face, even sadder than before. The voice said, "For more information, call the Maxatil Emergency Line." The number of Clay's law firm appeared across the bottom of the screen. The woman wiped a tear away from her eyes.

Everybody in the conference room clapped and cheered, then Clay sent them away to sit by their phones and start collecting clients. Within minutes, the calls started coming in. At nine o'clock, as scheduled, copies of the lawsuit were sent to newspapers and TV news channels. At ten o'clock, Clay was photographed by the press as he filed the lawsuit in the courthouse. By midday, Goffman shares had fallen to $61. The company hurriedly released a statement to the press, denying that Maxatil was dangerous and saying that it would defend the case energetically.

Patton French called at lunchtime. Clay was eating a sandwich while standing behind his desk and watching the phone messages pile up.

"I hope you know what you're doing," French warned him.

"I hope so, too, Patton. How are you?"

"Fine. We took a long hard look at Maxatil about six months ago, but decided not to proceed. Proving the link between the drug and cancer could be a real problem."

Clay dropped his sandwich and tried to breathe. He couldn't believe that Patton French had decided not to file a class-action lawsuit against one of the wealthiest companies in the country. Why? "Well, uh, Patton, we see things differently," he finally said, falling back into his chair.

"In fact, everybody decided to let it go, until you. A guy up in Chicago has a few cases, but he hasn't filed them yet. I don't know, maybe you're right. We weren't sure, that's all."

"We have evidence against them," Clay said, remembering the copy of the government report that Max Pace had said he had.

"You'd better be careful, Clay. Goffman are very good. They

make Ackerman Labs look like children."

"You sound scared, Patton. I'm surprised at you."

"Not scared at all. But if you make the smallest mistake, they'll eat you alive. And don't even think about a quick settlement."

"Will you join me in this lawsuit?"

"No. I didn't like it six months ago, and I don't like it now. Besides, I have too many other cases to deal with. Good luck."

Clay put down the phone and locked his office door. He walked to his window and stood for at least five minutes looking down at the traffic, rubbing the sweat from his forehead.


## Chapter 9   Dale Mooneyham

There was a lot of criticism of Clay in the next day's newspapers. They said that he was trying to bankrupt Goffman, one of America's finest companies, just to make more money for himself; they talked a lot about the $100 million he had already earned from mass tort cases the previous year, and demanded that the government should change the law to protect companies from high-earning lawyers like him.

Clay pretended to be amused by these stories. "A year ago no one was talking about me," he laughed to his colleagues. "Now they can't talk about me enough." But behind his locked office door, he felt anxious about the newspaper stories and worried about the speed of the lawsuit. He couldn't understand why no other lawyers seemed interested in suing Goffman.

Six days after the lawsuit had been filed, Max Pace telephoned from California.

"Tomorrow is the big day," he said.

"I need some good news," Clay said. "The government report?"

"I can't say," Pace replied. "And no more phone calls. Someone might be listening. I'll explain when I'm next in town."

Someone might be listening? Who? Why? Clay felt even more nervous and lost another night's sleep.

The following morning, the government report on Maxatil was published. It said that women who took Maxatil had a thirty-three percent higher risk of breast cancer and twenty-one percent higher risk of heart disease than women who didn't. It predicted that for every hundred thousand women using Maxatil for four years or more, four hundred would develop breast cancer and three hundred would suffer from heart disease. Goffman's shares fell immediately to $51, but there was no public response from the company. To Clay's relief, the next day's newspapers dropped their attacks on him, but he also felt ignored by them because they didn't support him either. He was delighted, however, to see the huge increase in phone calls from worried Maxatil patients.

♦

A week later, after spending two nights in Las Vegas with Ridley, Clay flew in his new Gulfstream jet to Tucson, Arizona, to discuss the Maxatil case with Dale Mooneyham. Mooneyham's offices were in an old, redecorated train station. In the reception area—the old station waiting room—two secretaries in their seventies sat quietly at their desks. One of them led Clay down a wide hall—its walls covered with framed newspaper reports of famous Dale Mooneyham courtroom victories—and into an enormous office where Dale Mooneyham himself was waiting behind a large desk. Mooneyham's handshake was cold and unfriendly; Clay wasn't welcome there, and he was confused by his reception. Mooneyham was at least seventy, a big man with a thick chest and large stomach, a long wide face, and the swollen eyes of a drinker. He had colored his gray hair black and wore blue jeans, bright red boots, and a cowboy shirt with no necktie.

"Nice office," Clay smiled, trying to be friendly.

"I bought it forty years ago for $5,000," Mooneyham replied.

"I saw all your newspaper cuttings outside."

"I've done all right, son. I haven't lost a jury trial in twenty years."

Clay glanced around and tried to relax in the low leather armchair. The office was at least five times bigger than his, with animal heads on the walls, no phones ringing, and no computers at all.

"I guess I'm here to talk about Maxatil," Clay eventually said.

Mooneyham narrowed his eyes slightly but was otherwise expressionless.

"It's a bad drug," he said simply. "I filed a lawsuit about five months ago in Flagstaff, so we should have a trial here by early fall. Unlike you, I don't file lawsuits until my case has been thoroughly investigated and prepared, and I'm ready to go to trial. If you do it that way, you always win your case. I've written a book about lawsuit preparation. You should read it."

"What about your client?" Clay asked.

"I just have one. I don't like class actions, at least not the way you and your friends handle them. Mass torts are a fraud, a form of robbery fueled by greed that one day will harm us all. Uncontroled greed will lead to the introduction of tighter laws and you boys will be out of business. But you won't care because you'll have all the money. The people who'll get harmed are all the future plaintiffs out there, all the little people who won't be able to sue for bad products because you boys have been too greedy."

"I asked about your client."

"Sixty-six-year-old white female, non-smoker, took Maxatil for four years. I met her a year ago. We take our time around here; we do our homework before we start shooting."

Clay had intended to talk about Maxatil in greater detail, but Mooneyham's attitude had instead made him want to leave as soon as possible.

"You're not expecting a settlement?" he asked, managing to sound interested.

"I don't settle, son. My clients know that about me. I take three cases a year, all carefully selected by me. I like different cases—products and theories I've never tried before, courthouses I've never seen. I get my choice because lawyers call me every day. And I always go to trial. I know that when I take a case it won't be settled. I tell all my clients that immediately. So that's good news for you, son, isn't it? If I'm successful, all of you can then advertise for more clients, settle them cheap, and make yourselves a fortune."

"I'd like to go to trial," Clay said.

"You've never worked in a big money trial before."

"I can learn."

Mooneyham shook his head and smiled. "You probably won't have to. When I've finished with Goffman, they'll run away from every jury."

"I don't have to settle."

"But you will. You'll have thousands of cases. You won't be brave enough to go to trial." He slowly stood, reached out a hand, and said, "I have work to do."

Clay hurried from the office, down the hall, through the reception area, and outside into the fierce desert heat.

## Chapter 10 The Hanna Portland Cement Company

The Hanna Portland Cement Company was started in Reedsburg, Pennsylvania, in 1946, and immediately became the largest employer in the small town. The Hanna brothers were strict employers, but they were fair to their workers, who were their neighbors as well. When business was good, the company was generous to its workers; when business was slow, everybody survived with less money. It was unusual for people to lose their jobs, and the contented workers never joined a union. All profits went back into the business and the community. The Hanna brothers built a hospital, a theater, and the nicest high school football field in the area. Over the years, they had received many attractive offers to buy the company, but they could never be sure that their factory would remain in Reedsburg. So they kept it. After fifty years of good management, the company employed four thousand of the eleven thousand residents in the town.

On the day the lawsuit arrived, Marcus Hanna, the boss of the company, was at a meeting with his cousin, Joel Hanna, the company lawyer. Joel read the lawsuit carefully and explained to his cousin that a number of homeowners were claiming damages over the poor quality cement that the company had manufactured three years earlier. Bricks were now falling off the houses that had been built with the cement. Marcus and Joel had already inspected several of the homes; they had calculated the number of possible claimants at five hundred, and the cost of repairing each home at $12,000. They hadn't been too worried because their insurance would cover the first $5 million of any claim. But, according to the lawsuit that Joel was now reading, two thousand homeowners were suing the company for $25,000 each. Their attorney was Clay Carter.

"That's $50 million!" Marcus said with disbelief.

"And their lawyer will take forty percent of it," added Joel.

"He can't do that," Marcus said.

"They do it every day."

♦

On May 1st, Rex Crittle left the accounting firm where he had worked for eighteen years and became Clay's business manager. With the offer of a huge increase in salary and benefits, he simply couldn't say no. The day after Crittle moved in, Rodney moved out, although the two events weren't related. Rodney had had enough of the pressure at work and wanted to spend more time with his family. With $10 million in his bank account, he could afford to. Clay was sad to see him go, but the truth was that he no longer needed someone like Rodney. The firm needed energetic, highly-educated young lawyers, not ordinary paralegals like Rodney.

Later that month, Patton French ordered a meeting of the Dyloft Plaintiffs' Guidance Committee, and Clay flew down to Biloxi with Ridley in his new jet. Patton French welcomed them both onto his two-hundred-foot luxury boat in shorts. While Ridley and the other wives and girlfriends relaxed in the sun, the conversation among the lawyers soon turned to Maxatil and Clay's lawsuit against Goffman.

"I have a thousand Maxatil cases," Carlos, one of the lawyers said, "but I'm not sure what to do with them. I haven't filed them yet. Proving the link between the drug and cancer could be almost impossible."

"I still don't like it," French added. "I was talking to a friend of mine in Dallas. He has two thousand cases, and isn't sure what to do with them either."

"The problem," Carlos said, "is that the diseases caused by Maxatil have many other possible causes as well. I've had four experts study this drug. They all say that when a woman is taking Maxatil and gets breast cancer, it's impossible to link the disease to the drug."

"Have you had any reaction from Goffman?" French asked Clay, who wasn't enjoying this conversation.

"Nothing," he said. "I think we're all waiting for Mooneyham."

"I talked to him yesterday," said Wes Saulsberry, the lawyer who had told Clay about the Hanna Portland Cement Company. "I know Mooneyham very well. We tried some cases together years ago. He's very good. Everybody's watching Mooneyham. Even Goffman. The trial is set for sometime in September. If Mooneyham can prove the link between Maxatil and breast cancer, Goffman will almost certainly set up a national compensation plan. But if the jury agrees with Goffman, then it will be war because the company won't pay a cent to anybody."

"That's what Mooneyham says?" French said, shaking his head dismissively. "The man's all show and no substance."

"No, I've heard it, too," Carlos said. "I have a source who says exactly the same thing as Wes."

"I've never heard of a defendant wanting a trial," French said.

"Goffman's tough," a third lawyer added. "I sued them fifteen years ago. If you can prove your case, they'll pay a fair settlement. But if you can't, you're in big trouble."

Clay was feeling worse and worse but, fortunately for him, Maxatil was immediately forgotten when the conversation turned to the Guidance Committee's latest fee schedule. Clay would soon be receiving another $4 million from the Dyloft settlement. Good news: it would stop Rex Crittle, his firm's business manager, complaining—at least for a few more weeks.

♦

For several days, Joel Hanna had considered working alone. He would present the company's survival plan; he really needed no help doing this since it was his own original idea. But Babcock, the attorney for their insurance company, insisted on being present. His client had insured the Hanna Portland Cement Company for $5 million, so Joel couldn't stop him. Together they walked into Clay's luxurious law offices. Clay kept them waiting for a short time before rushing into the conference room, jacket over his shoulder, showing everyone that he was a very busy man. Joel Hanna was impressed, and couldn't help thinking, *This guy made $100 million last year.* Babcock had the same thought, but he also remembered that, despite all his money, Clay had never tried a civil lawsuit, and had never asked a jury for a cent. He was sure that he saw signs of nervousness beneath Clay's surface confidence.

"You said you had a plan," Clay said. "Let's hear it."

The survival plan was simple. The company was willing to admit, for the purposes of this meeting only, that it had manufactured some bad cement and that, because of this, a number of new homes in Baltimore would have to be re-bricked. They were willing to compensate the homeowners, but they had no intention of bankrupting their own company. The company was short of cash, but was willing to borrow heavily to compensate the victims. "This is our mistake, and we intend to correct it," Joel Hanna said more than once.

"Do you know how many homes need compensating?" Clay asked.

"Nine hundred and twenty-two," Joel said.

Clay wrote some figures in his note book, then looked up and said, "So if we assume a cost of $25,000 for each client, we're looking at just over 23 million."

"We're sure that it will cost a lot less than that to fix each house," Joel said.

"We have statements from four building firms in the Howard County area," Clay replied. "The average estimate for repair to the damage is $20,000."

"I'd like to see those estimates," Joel said.

"Maybe later. Plus, there are other damages. These homeowners need to be compensated for inconvenience, loss of enjoyment, and the effect on their health. One of our clients is suffering from severe headaches over this. Another lost a profitable sale on his home because the bricks were falling off."

"We have estimates closer to twelve thousand," Joel said.

"We're not going to settle these cases for $12,000," Clay said.

Fifteen thousand dollars was a fair figure and would get new bricks on every house. But such a settlement left only $9,000 for the client after Clay had taken his thirty-three percent. Ten thousand dollars would not be enough to finish the job. Clay did the math quickly: at $15,000 for each claim, Hanna would need about $15 million. $5 million would come from its insurance; it could borrow the rest—but this was only the first meeting. This wasn't the time to make any decisions.

The final result would all depend on how much money Clay wanted to make. If he reduced his percentage, he would still make several million dollars, protect his clients, and allow Hanna Portland Cement, a fine old company, to survive. Or, if he insisted on his thirty-three percent, everybody would suffer.

## Chapter 11    Reasons to be Anxious

Miss Glick sounded a little nervous. "There are two of them, Clay," she said, almost in a whisper. "FBI.*"

Clay's first reaction was surprise, but then he relaxed and laughed to himself. He had certainly done nothing wrong. He asked the two policemen to come into his office.

"Do you know a man by the name of Martin Grace?" the first man, Agent Spooner, began.

"No."

"Mike Packer?" asked the second man, Agent Lohse.

"No."

"Max Pace?"

"Yes."

"They're all the same person," Spooner said. "Have you any

---

* FBI: the criminal investigation agency working for the U.S. Department of Justice

idea where we can find him?"

"No."

"When did you last see him?"

Clay considered his answer for a long time—he needed time to organize his thoughts. He didn't have to answer their questions. He could ask them to leave and come back when he had a lawyer present. If they mentioned Tarvan, he would end the meeting immediately.

"I'm not sure," he said. "It's been several months. Some time in mid-February."

"Where did you meet him?" Spooner asked, while Lohse made notes.

"Dinner in his hotel."

"Which hotel?"

"I don't remember. Why are you interested in Max Pace?"

"Pace has a history of fraud and dishonest dealing in shares. We're interviewing witnesses. We know he spent some time in D.C. We know he visited you on Mustique last Christmas. We know that in January he sold a lot of Goffman shares at $62 the day before you filed your big lawsuit, and bought them back at $49, making himself a profit of several million. We think he had a secret government report on a Goffman drug called Maxatil, and he used that information to commit serious fraud."

"Anything else?"

"Did you sell any Goffman shares before you filed your lawsuit against them?"

"I did not."

"Have you ever owned Goffman shares?"

"No."

Lohse put his pen in his pocket, and the two policemen stood and headed for the door.

"If you hear from Pace, we'd like to know about it," Spooner said.

"Don't be too optimistic," Clay said. He could never betray Pace because of all the secrets they shared.

"We're always optimistic, Mr. Clay. On our next visit, we'll talk about Ackerman Labs. Goodbye."

♦

Just as Clay was leaving his office one night, Rex Crittle walked in with a sour look on his face and said, "Our insurance company has informed us that they're canceling their cover for this firm."

"What!" Clay shouted. "Why?"

"They don't like what they see. Twenty-four thousand Maxatil cases scares them. Their $10 million won't be enough to cover the losses if something goes wrong, so they're canceling the contract."

"Can they do that?"

"Of course they can. An insurance company can cancel its contract whenever it wants. We're in danger, Clay. We have no insurance."

"We don't need insurance."

"I'm still worried."

"You were also worried about Dyloft, as I recall."

"And I was wrong."

"Well, Rex, you're wrong about Maxatil, too. After Mr. Mooneyham has finished with Goffman in Flagstaff, they'll be anxious to settle. Our twenty-four thousand cases are worth a billion dollars, Rex. And Goffman can afford it."

"What if something goes wrong?"

"Stop worrying. After the Mooneyham trial in September, the money will soon come pouring in again."

With those words, Clay smiled, picked up his jacket, gave Crittle a friendly pat on the shoulder, and left for dinner.

Clay had arranged to have dinner with an old college friend

but, while he was waiting at the bar, the friend called him on his cell phone to say he was unable to come. As Clay was leaving, he glanced into the restaurant and saw Rebecca having dinner with two other women. He stepped back and ordered another beer. He wanted desperately to talk to Rebecca, but he was determined not to be a nuisance. A trip to the rest room would work fine.

As he walked by her table, she looked up and immediately smiled. Rebecca introduced Clay to her two friends, and he explained that he was waiting for an old college friend for dinner. The guy was late, he might have to wait for a long time, and he apologized for the interruption.

Fifteen minutes later, Rebecca appeared in the crowded bar and stood close beside him.

"I just have a minute," she said. "They're waiting." She nodded toward her friends in the restaurant.

"You look great," Clay told her.

"You, too."

"Where's your husband?"

"Working," she sighed. "He's always working."

"How's married life?"

"Very lonely," she said, looking away.

Clay took a drink. If she hadn't been in a crowded bar with friends waiting for her, Clay knew she would have told him a lot more. *The marriage isn't working!* Clay struggled to hide a smile. "I'm still waiting," he said.

Her eyes were wet when she leaned over and kissed him on the cheek. Then she was gone without another word.

♦

One afternoon, sitting in front of the baseball on TV, Ted Worley fell asleep in his armchair, which wasn't unusual for him. What was unusual was that he woke up after one hour instead of the usual two, and that he felt a desperate need for the toilet. He walked to the small guest bathroom down the hall, closed the door behind him, unzipped his pants, and began to urinate. A very slight burning sensation caused him to glance down, and when he did he almost fainted. His urine was the color of rust—a dark red liquid. He leaned one hand against the wall to stop himself from falling. When he finished, he sat on the toilet seat for a few minutes to collect his thoughts.

"What are you doing in there?" his wife called from the bedroom next door.

"None of your business," he shouted angrily.

"Are you OK, Ted?"

"I'm fine."

But he wasn't fine. He lifted the lid, looked again at the bloody urine in the bowl, pulled the handle, and walked slowly back to his armchair in front of the TV. But he couldn't concentrate on the baseball. Twenty minutes later, after three glasses of water, he went down to the basement and urinated in a small bathroom, as far away from his wife as possible.

It was blood, he decided. The tumors were back, and they were far more serious than they had been before.

He told his wife the truth the next morning, over breakfast, and she immediately made an appointment for him at the hospital. Four days later, malignant tumors were found in Mr. Worley's bladder. During five hours of surgery, the doctors removed all the tumors they could find.

The senior specialist at the hospital was watching Mr. Worley very carefully. A colleague at a hospital in Kansas City had reported a similar case a month earlier: the appearance of malignant tumors in the bladder of a former Dyloft plaintiff. The patient in Kansas City was having treatment, but he didn't have much longer to live.

The same could be expected for Mr. Worley, although the

specialist tried to sound optimistic on his first visit after the operation. Mr. Worley would be allowed out of the hospital in a week's time, and, as soon as he was strong enough, they would begin aggressively treating his cancer.

Later, the specialist learned of another similar case in another hospital. All three patients had been Dyloft plaintiffs. Now they were dying. A lawyer's name was mentioned. The Kansas City patient was represented by a small firm in New York City.

It was a rare and rewarding experience for a doctor to be able to pass along the name of one lawyer who would sue another. Mr. Worley's specialist was determined to enjoy the moment. He entered Mr. Worley's room and talked to him about the Dyloft case and the small settlement.

"I was against the settlement," Mr. Worley said. "I wrote two angry letters to the lawyer who filed the lawsuit against Ackerman Labs, Mr. Clay Carter, but got no reply."

"I guess it's too late now," Mrs. Worley added tearfully.

"Maybe not," the doctor said. He told them about the Kansas City patient, a man very similar to Ted Worley. "He's hired a lawyer to sue *his* lawyer," the doctor said.

"I've had enough of lawyers," Mr. Worley said.

"Do you have his number?" Mrs. Worley asked. She was thinking much more clearly than her husband. Sadly, she was already thinking about the future, after her husband had gone.

The specialist had the number.

♦

Helen Warshaw was a lawyer who specialized in suing mass tort lawyers for bad settlements. It was her job to threaten them with court unless they settled quickly—and guilty lawyers *always* settled quickly! No one avoided a courtroom with as much energy as a tort lawyer caught making too much money for himself and not enough for his client.

Helen already had four Dyloft cases in her New York office when she received the call from Mrs. Worley. Her firm had a small file on Clay Carter and a much thicker one on Patton French. After a few minutes on the phone with Mrs. Worley, Helen knew exactly what had happened.

"I'll be there by five o'clock," she said.

Helen flew to Dulles then rented a car—no private jets for her!—to drive to the hospital in Bethesda. Mrs. Worley had collected their papers, which Helen studied carefully while Mr. Worley slept. When he woke up, he didn't want to talk. He didn't trust lawyers, especially aggressive, female, New York lawyers. However, his wife had plenty of time and found it easier to talk to a woman. The two went to the lounge for coffee and a long discussion, during which Helen told Mrs. Worley that, although she couldn't sue Ackerman Labs or the doctor who supplied her husband with Dyloft, she could still sue the attorney who had agreed the final settlement between the plaintiffs and the company.

A week later, Helen Warshaw filed a lawsuit against J. Clay Carter, F. Patton French, M. Wesley Saulsberry, and all the other known and unknown attorneys who had agreed inadequate settlements with Ackerman Labs. The principal plaintiff was, again, Mr. Ted Worley. Fifteen minutes after the lawsuit was filed, Helen sent copies of it to a dozen important newspapers.

## Chapter 12    Sued and Investigated

The reporters were already calling by the time Clay finished reading the class action.

"I've never heard of this," he said quietly to Oscar Mulrooney, a young, ambitious lawyer who had become his closest friend at the firm since Jonah, Rodney, and Paulette had left. He was aware that there was much he didn't know about the mass tort game. He had had no idea that Ted Worley was sick again. There hadn't been a sign of trouble anywhere in the country. It just wasn't fair.

Oscar was too shocked to speak.

Miss Glick called through to say that a reporter from the *Washington Post* was waiting to speak to him.

"Tell him I'm not here and call security!" Clay shouted angrily.

Clay and Oscar discussed the problem for a long time, but couldn't decide what to do. Finally, Oscar volunteered to break the news to the rest of the staff.

"If I'm wrong, I'll pay the claim," Clay said.

"Let's hope Mr. Worley is the only one suing this firm."

"That's the big question, Oscar. How many Ted Worleys are out there?"

That night, Clay couldn't sleep. His thoughts were on Ted Worley. He wasn't angry—his former client wouldn't be claiming to have malignant tumors if they didn't actually exist. Mr. Worley's cancer was caused by a bad drug, not a bad lawyer, but who could blame the man for being angry with him? To settle a case hurriedly for $62,000 when it was really worth millions showed a mixture of bad professional practice and greed. Clay tried to think about other things, but all thoughts eventually came back to Mr. Worley, a client who had not been protected by his lawyer. The sense of guilt was so heavy that he felt like calling the man and apologizing. Maybe he would write him a letter. He clearly remembered the two letters that Mr. Worley had written him. He and Jonah had laughed about them.

Soon after 4 A.M., Clay made a pot of coffee and read the news on the Internet. One of the headlines was: MASS TORT LAWYER IS SUED BY THE MASSES. Clay read the report, and other similar reports, all celebrating the fact that a rich tort lawyer was in serious trouble, and felt sick, realizing that he could expect no sympathy, no defenders. An unknown source estimated the number of plaintiffs at a dozen. Many more plaintiffs were expected to follow. *How many?* Clay asked himself as he made more coffee. *How many Ted Worleys are out there?*

At seven o'clock, Clay was at work, pretending to be cheerful, laughing and joking with the staff, but Miss Glick spoiled his good humor by stepping into his office and saying, "Clay, those two FBI agents are back."

"Wonderful!" he said, with a big but very false smile.

Spooner and Lohse looked serious and they didn't shake his hand. Clay closed the door with the same false smile, and told himself to keep performing. But the strain and constant fear was beginning to tire him.

"Any news of your friend Pace?" Lohse began.

"No."

"Are you sure?"

"Are you deaf?" Clay replied sharply. "I said no."

"We think he was in the city last week."

"I haven't seen him."

"You filed a lawsuit against Ackerman on July 2nd of last year, correct?"

"Yes."

"Did you own any shares in the company before you filed the lawsuit?"

"No."

"Did you sell the shares for a high price, then buy them back at a lower price?"

Of course he had. His good friend Max Pace had advised him to. They knew the answer to the question. They had the data, he was sure of that. Since their first visit, he had been thoroughly investigated for fraud and dishonest trading. He was in trouble. He shouldn't have dealt the shares.

"Am I under investigation for something?" he asked.

"Yes," Lohse nodded.

"Then this meeting is at an end. My attorney will be in touch with you." Clay was on his feet and heading for the door.

♦

The atmosphere at the next meeting of the Dyloft Plaintiffs' Guidance Committee was very tense as soon as Clay entered the room. The lawyers were scared, and with good reason. "New people are joining the class action against us all the time," one of the lawyers said. "Seven of my Dyloft plaintiffs are suffering from malignant tumors already."

"And Warshaw is a dangerous woman," Wes Saulsberry added, the others nodding in agreement. Everybody, apart from Clay, seemed to know about her. "She never settles. She always wants trials—big, exciting trials that fill the front pages of all the newspapers."

"You now have seven plaintiffs suing you," French said, handing Clay a list of names. "I'm told by my source at Ackerman that we can expect the list to grow."

Clay looked at the list of names. Apart from Ted Worley, he didn't recognize any of them.

"Is there any hope that we can prove this cancer isn't linked to Dyloft?" Saulsberry asked.

"No. We're in big trouble," French replied sharply.

"If the medical information is accurate, there's no way we can defend these cases," Saulsberry said, saying what was already obvious.

The discussion continued, but Clay wasn't listening. He was working out how much he would have to pay to compensate the seven plaintiffs on his list. If he gave them $3 million each, he would have to pay over $20 million, which he could manage. But if the list kept growing …

♦

Clay had interviewed hundreds of nervous clients in his time as a lawyer at OPD, but now it was *his* turn to feel nervous when he walked into the office of Zack Battle, his defense lawyer. At $750 an hour, Clay wanted the meeting to be as short as possible. Clay told him the Dyloft story, beginning with Max Pace and ending with the FBI. He didn't talk about Tarvan, but he would if it became necessary. Strangely, Battle took no notes. He just listened, frowning and smoking his pipe, sometimes staring into the distance but never betraying what he thought. Eventually, he asked, "Did you have the information that Max Pace had stolen when you sold your Ackerman shares and filed the lawsuit?"

"Of course. I had to know that I could prove the connection between Dyloft and the development of tumors if we went to trial."

"Then that's dishonest trading. You're guilty. Five years in jail. Tell me, though, how the FBI can prove it."

"Max Pace can tell them, I guess."

"Who else has the secret information?"

"Patton French, maybe one or two of the other guys."

"Does Patton French know that you had this information before you filed the lawsuit?"

"I don't know. I never told him when I got it."

"So if the FBI can't find Max Pace, you're safe. If they don't know you had this secret information when you sold your Ackerman shares, they can't arrest you for dishonest trading. They know when and for how much you sold them, but that's not enough. They have to prove you had the knowledge. I suggest you go and see Patton French, make sure the secret information on Dyloft can't be traced back to you. Don't talk to anyone else about this case—the FBI are probably watching you very carefully. And, most importantly, pray that Max Pace is either dead or hiding in Europe."

♦

The letter had been sent from a prison. Although he had many former clients behind bars, Clay couldn't remember one called Paul Watson. He opened the envelope and pulled out a one-page letter, very neatly typed. It read:

*Dear Mr Carter: You may remember me as Tequila Watson. I've changed my name because I don't like the old one any more. I read the Bible every day and my favorite guy in it is called Paul, so I've borrowed his name. I need a favor. Could you contact Pumpkin's family and tell them that I'm very sorry for what happened? I've prayed to God and he has forgiven me. I would feel much better if Pumpkin's family could do the same. I still can't believe I killed him like that. It wasn't me doing the shooting, but the devil, I guess. But I have no excuses.*

*I'm still not taking drugs. It would be great if you could write to me. I don't get much mail. Sorry you had to stop being my lawyer. I liked you. Best wishes,*

*Paul Watson*

"Be patient," Clay smiled to himself as he put down the letter. "If things continue like this, I'll be joining you in prison very soon."

## Chapter 13   More Angry Plaintiffs

The next day, Clay was in the newspapers again. There were pictures of him under the headline: KING OF TORTS UNDER FBI INVESTIGATION. Clay was beginning to feel lonely. He received only one call, from an old college friend, trying to make him feel better. He appreciated the call, but it did little to help his mood. Where were his other friends?

He tried not to, but he couldn't stop thinking about Rebecca and the Van Horns. What were they thinking about him now? He didn't care, he told himself again and again. But if he didn't care, why couldn't he stop thinking about them?

♦

The next meeting between Joel Hanna and Clay would be the last, although neither Clay nor anyone on his side of the table realized it. Joel Hanna brought his cousin Marcus, the company's boss, with him, and left behind Babcock, the attorney for their insurance company.

"We've found an additional eighteen homes that should be added to the list," Joel began the discussion. "That makes a total of nine hundred and forty. We feel very confident that there won't be any more."

"That's good," Clay smiled.

A longer list meant more clients for him, more compensation to be paid by the Hanna company. Ninety percent of the homeowners were Clay's clients. His team had assured them that they would get more money because Mr. Carter was an expert at mass litigation.

During the last meeting, Clay had reduced his demands from $25,000 per claim to $22,500, a settlement that would bring in fees of $7.5 million. The Hanna company was only willing to pay $17,000, which was its maximum borrowing capacity. At $17,000 per home, Clay would earn about $4.8 million in fees, if he insisted on taking thirty percent of the settlement. If, however, he cut his share to twenty percent, each of his clients would make $13,600. This would reduce his fees by $1.5 million. Marcus Hanna had found a builder who would agree to repair every home for $13,500.

However, since the last meeting, there had been several stories about Clay in the newspapers, and none of them were good. In addition to this, Clay's firm wasn't bringing in any money. He had stopped advertising for new Maxatil clients, Rex Crittle was trying to cut costs, and the number of former Dyloft clients joining Helen Warshaw in suing him was growing. A reduction in fees, therefore, wasn't something that his firm was prepared to discuss.

"Any change in your position?" Clay asked.

Instead of just saying no, Joel explained the financial difficulties that his company was facing.

"So there's no change?" Clay asked when Joel had finished.

"No. $17,000 per person is as high as we can go."

"We want $22,500," Clay said calmly. "If you're not moving, then neither are we." His voice was as hard as steel.

His staff were impressed by his toughness, but also anxious for him to moderate his demands. But Clay was thinking of how Patton French had behaved in the discussions with the men from Ackerman Labs. He firmly believed that if he kept pushing, Hanna would surrender to his demands.

But he was wrong. Without warning, Marcus Hanna said, "Well, then it's time to go." He and his cousin collected their papers and walked angrily out of the conference room.

Two hours later, the Hanna Portland Cement Company formally declared itself bankrupt, unable to pay any of its debts. The plaintiffs in the class action filed against it by J. Clay Carter of Washington, D.C., would now not be receiving any money at all.

♦

The *Baltimore Press* published a long, detailed story about the bankruptcy and the immediate reaction by the homeowners— evidence that someone very close to the settlement discussions was whispering to the reporter. The company had offered $17,000 per plaintiff; repairs to each home were estimated at $15,000. The lawsuit could have been fairly settled if the attorneys' fees hadn't been so high.

The plaintiffs were extremely unhappy. "We should've dealt directly with Hanna," one of them complained to the reporter. "Can we sue the lawyer? I tried calling him, but the lines are busy," said another. "We didn't want the company to go bankrupt," said a third.

The reporter continued by giving information about Clay Carter's background, including his involvement with the Dyloft fees. Things got worse from there. Three photographs helped tell the story: the first was a homeowner pointing to the bricks falling out of her house; the second was a group meeting of homeowners in a garage; the third was Clay and Ridley standing in front of the White House before the state dinner. Underneath it were the words: "Mr. Carter, seen above at a White House dinner, could not be reached for comment."

"Yes, that's right," Clay thought, throwing the paper onto his desk. "I'm not talking to *anyone*!"

Clay spent the day locked in his office, avoiding all calls. Then, in the afternoon, the sound of shouting reached him from the hallway, where the security guard was trying to control a very angry man.

"Where is Clay Carter?" the man shouted.

"Here!" Clay shouted back, coming out of his office. "What do you want?"

"I'm one of your clients," the man said, breathing heavily, the security guard gripping his arms.

"Let him go," Clay told the guard.

"I'd like a conference with my attorney," the man said.

"This is not the way to schedule one," Clay replied calmly.

"Yeah, well, I tried the other way but all the lines are busy. You robbed us of a good settlement with the cement company. We want to know why. Not enough money for you?"

"I guess you believe everything you read in the newspapers," Clay said.

"I believe we've been robbed by our own lawyer. And we're not accepting it without a fight."

"You need to relax and stop worrying. We're still working on the settlement," Clay lied.

"Cut your fees and get us some money," the man said angrily.

"I'll get you a settlement," Clay said with a false smile. "Just relax."

When the man had left, Clay turned to the rest of his staff and clapped his hands. "Back to work everybody," he said cheerfully.

An hour later, Clay had a surprise visitor: Rebecca. Clay eagerly invited her into his office, where they sat for a long time without talking. Finally, Rebecca said, "Clay, are you OK? There's so much bad publicity about you. I'm worried about you."

"So you haven't forgotten all about me?"

"No, I haven't. I still think about you."

"All the time?"

"Yes, more and more."

"How's the worm?" Clay asked, referring to her husband.

"He's OK," she replied, not angry with his question.

"You don't seem very happy with him," Clay said, looking at her hopefully.

Rebecca avoided answering by asking Clay a question of her own: "How's your girlfriend, Clay?"

"I think she prefers girls to men." They both laughed for a long time. And then they were silent again, because there was so much to say.

"Are you going to survive?" Rebecca finally asked.

"Let's not talk about me. Let's talk about us."

"I'm married," she said.

"But a relationship would be fun, wouldn't it?"

"Maybe, but I'm not going to live like that."

"I'm not either, Rebecca. I'm not sharing. I'll wait until you're single again. But would you hurry up and leave him?"

"That might not happen, Clay."

"Yes it will."

## Chapter 14   Under Attack

The day before the trial inside the Coconino County Courthouse in Flagstaff, the atmosphere was tense. On one side of the room sat Dale Mooneyham and his team; on the other sat the huge Goffman team, led by a well-known, experienced lawyer from L.A., Roger Redding. He was known as Roger the Rocket, because he struck fast and hard.

Clay and Oscar Mulrooney watched from the back of the courtroom as the lawyers argued with each other over technical details. Mooneyham moved slowly around the courtroom, leaning heavily on a stick and shouting at the judge and Roger Redding in his rich, deep voice. Redding, in contrast, was calm and relaxed, speaking quietly in beautifully-structured sentences, making even the most complex arguments easy to understand. He wasn't afraid of Dale Mooneyham.

During a fifteen-minute break, Clay went outside to find something cold to drink. On his way back to the courtroom, a reporter stepped in front of him. He was Derek somebody, from the *Financial Weekly*, and he wanted a quick word or two.

"Can I ask you what you're doing here?" Derek said.

"I guess you can," Clay said with suspicion. He knew the *Financial Weekly*—it hated all lawyers, especially mass-tort lawyers like him.

"What are you doing here?"

"The same thing you're doing here."

"And that is?"

"Enjoying the heat."

"Is it true you have twenty-five thousand Maxatil cases?"

"No."

"How many?"

"Twenty-six thousand."

"How much are they worth?"

"Somewhere between zero and a couple of billion dollars."

Unknown to Clay, the judge had banned the lawyers from both sides from talking to the media until the end of the trial. Clay attracted a large crowd because of his willingness to talk. He was surprised to see himself surrounded by reporters. He answered a few more questions without saying much at all.

The next day the *Arizona Ledger* quoted him as claiming his cases could be worth $2 billion. It had a photograph of Clay outside the courtroom, microphones in his face, with the words "KING OF TORTS IN TOWN" underneath it. The accompanying report gave a brief summary of Clay's visit and a few words about the big trial itself. The reporter didn't directly call him a greedy, money-loving lawyer who made a fortune out of people's suffering, but he implied it.

At 9 A.M. the courtroom was crowded with people, but there was no sign of the lawyers or the judge. A young man in a suit stopped in front of where Clay was sitting, leaned forward, and whispered: "Are you Mr. Carter?"

Clay nodded with surprise.

"The judge would like to see you."

The newspaper was in the middle of the judge's desk. Dale Mooneyham was in one corner of the large office. Roger Redding was leaning on a table by the window. The judge was rocking in his chair. None of the three looked happy. Very awkward introductions were made. Mooneyham refused to step forward and shake Clay's hand.

"Are you aware that I have banned lawyers from talking to

the media, Mr. Carter?" asked the judge.

"No, sir."

"Well, I have."

"I'm not one of the attorneys in this case."

"We work hard at having fair trials in Arizona, Mr. Carter. Both sides want a fair-minded jury. Now, thanks to you, the people on the jury know that there are at least twenty-six thousand similar cases out there."

Clay had no intention of appearing weak or apologizing in front of Roger Redding, whom he might have to fight in future legal battles. "Maybe it was unavoidable," he said.

"Why don't you just leave Arizona?" Mooneyham shouted from the corner.

"I really don't have to," Clay replied sharply.

"You want me to lose?"

Clay had heard enough. He wasn't sure how his presence might harm Mooneyham's case, but he didn't want to take any unnecessary risks. He looked at Roger Redding and said, "See you in D.C."

Redding smiled politely, but slowly shook his head.

Oscar Mulrooney agreed to remain in Flagstaff and watch the trial. Clay boarded his private jet and flew home.

♦

In Reedsburg, the news that twelve hundred workers were losing their jobs at Hanna brought the town to a halt. In a letter to all his employees, Marcus Hanna explained why the company had gone bankrupt—the failure to reach a settlement in the class-action lawsuit. The company had tried to reach a fair, honest agreement, but a greedy law firm in D.C. had made unreasonable demands. The *Baltimore Press* reported the story, and openly blamed Clay for all of Reedsburg's misery: the company would not have gone bankrupt if he had not demanded such high fees.

When Clay read the report, he wanted to sue the newspaper.

However, he soon had bigger problems to worry about. There was a two-page article in *Newsweek* about Helen Warshaw. Clay had never seen Ms. Warshaw before; when he saw the photo of her standing in front of an empty jury box somewhere, looking attractive and successful, he hoped that he never would.

The article described how Ms. Warshaw was one of three partners in a New York firm that specialized in dishonest legal practice. Now, she was ready to do battle with some of the biggest and richest lawyers in the country, and she wasn't going to settle. She had fifty Dyloft clients, all dying, all suing. There was an interview with Mr. Ted Worley, who gave the magazine his full story. "I didn't want to settle," he said more than once. For *Newsweek*, Ted Worley produced all his paperwork, including copies of the two letters of protest he had written to Clay Carter and to which he had never received a reply.

According to his doctors, Ted Worley had less than six months to live. Slowly reading each awful word of the story, Clay felt as if he was responsible for the cancer. He threw the magazine across the floor. He wished that he had never met Ted Worley, never met Max Pace, never even thought about going to law school.

He called his pilots and told them to get his private jet ready.

"Where to, sir?"

"Biloxi, Mississippi."

"One person or two?"

"Just me." He hadn't seen Ridley for two days and he had no desire to take her with him. He needed time away from the city and anything that reminded him of it.

He spent two days on French's boat, from which he followed the Maxatil trial with the help of emails from Oscar Mulrooney. Choosing the jury had taken one whole day, and Dale Mooneyham was now slowly presenting the plaintiff's case against the drug. The government study was powerful evidence. The jury was extremely interested in it.

"Things are going well," Oscar wrote. "Mooneyham is an excellent performer, but Redding has better courtroom skills."

Late on the second afternoon, after a couple of drinks on the deck, French asked Clay, "How much cash do you have left?"

"I don't know—20 million maybe."

"And how much insurance?"

"Ten million. They canceled it, but they're still insuring me for Dyloft."

French sucked on a lemon and said, "I'm not sure 30 million is enough for you. You have twenty-one Dyloft claims now, and the number can only go up. We'll be lucky if we can settle them for 3 million each."

"How many cases do you have?"

"Nineteen."

"And how much cash do you have?"

"Two hundred million. I'll be all right."

After a long silence, Clay asked, "What happens if Goffman wins in Flagstaff? I have all these cases."

"You'll be in big trouble. How much have you spent on Maxatil?"

"Eight million just in advertising."

"I suggest you think positive. Mooneyham hasn't lost a case for a long time. If he wins easily, Goffman will have to think about settling. If he wins narrowly, they'll probably want to take you to court and try again. You can hire a top lawyer and still beat them."

"You wouldn't advise me to try it myself?"

"No. You don't have the experience. It takes years in the courtroom before you're ready for a big trial like this."

◆

At eight thirty on Saturday evening, Clay was getting ready to meet Jonah, who was back in town, for dinner when the telephone rang.

"Is this Clay Carter?" a male voice asked.

"Yes," Clay replied as he was buttoning his shirt. "Who is this?"

"I'm from Reedsburg, Pennsylvania, and I have some valuable information about the Hanna company."

Clay's blood ran cold. He sat on the edge of his bed, trying to think clearly. "OK, I'm listening," he said at last.

"We can't talk over the phone," the voice said. "It's a long story. There are some papers."

"Where are you?"

"I'm in the city. I'll meet you inside the entrance of the Four Seasons Hotel. We can talk there."

"When?" Clay asked.

"I'll be there in five minutes. How long will it take you?"

"Ten minutes."

"Good. I'm wearing jeans and a black baseball cap."

"I'll find you," Clay said, then hung up.

He finished dressing and hurried out of his town house. Walking rapidly along Dumbarton, he tried to imagine what information he could need or even want from the Hanna company. He turned south on Thirty-first Street, lost in thought. A lady passed with a small dog. A young man in a black jacket with a cigarette hanging from his mouth approached, although Clay barely noticed him. As the man passed him, in front of a poorly lit town house and under the branches of an old tree, he suddenly, with perfect timing and accuracy, lifted his fist and hit Clay on the chin.

Clay never saw it. He remembered a sudden pain in his face, and his head crashing into an iron fence. Another man joined the first and they both started hitting and kicking Clay as he lay on the ground. Clay rolled onto his side and managed to get to his knees, then a heavy stick landed like a gunshot on the back of his head.

He heard a woman's voice in the distance, then he lost consciousness.

The lady who had been walking her dog saw two men in black jackets hitting a man lying on the ground with large black sticks, and screamed. The men ran away, and she dialled 911* on her cell phone. She tried to assist the young man on the ground, who was unconscious and bleeding badly.

Clay was taken to George Washington University Hospital, where initial examination revealed two large head wounds and several other cuts and bruises. A bone in his right leg was cracked neatly in two, his left kneecap was in pieces, and the left ankle was broken. Eighty-one stitches were required to close two large cuts in his head. After smaller cuts in his cheek and ear had been stitched, he was taken into surgery to have his legs put back together.

Jonah began calling after waiting impatiently for thirty minutes. He left the restaurant after an hour and walked angrily to Clay's town house. He knocked on the door, rang the bell, and was ready to leave when he saw Clay's car parked in the street. He walked slowly toward it. Something was wrong, although he wasn't sure what. It was a black Porsche Carrera, but it was covered with white dust. He called the police.

A torn and empty Hanna Portland Cement bag was found under the Porsche. Someone seemed to have covered the car with cement, then thrown water at it. After a long computer search, Jonah found Clay's name and hurried to the hospital. Clay was in surgery when he arrived, but it was only broken bones. His injuries didn't seem to be life-threatening.

At 1:30 A.M., a doctor reported to Jonah that the surgery had gone smoothly. "He looks awful," she warned him. Jonah finally managed to see Clay two hours later in a private room that he had arranged. Clay was covered from head to foot in thick bandages, his legs held six inches above the bed by a complex

* 911: the phone number for emergency services in the United States

series of cables. He was still unconscious, and his eyes, chin, and lips were blue and swollen. Blood had dried on his neck.

Jonah watched him quietly for several minutes and then started to smile. "Look at him," he said to himself. "There lies the King of Torts." And, to the horror of the nurses, he shook with laughter.


## Chapter 15   The Goffman Case

The story was in all the newspapers on Monday morning, and later that same day Ridley arrived. She showed great affection for a few minutes and tried to interest Clay in details of how she was having the house on Mustique decorated. Clay soon had a terrible headache and asked for a pill. A few minutes later he fell asleep, and when he awoke she was gone.

Over the next few days, the swelling began to go down and he was able to think more clearly. He stopped taking pain pills so that he could concentrate more on running the office by phone and email on the laptop computer that Jonah had brought him. He was also finally able to pay attention to Oscar Mulrooney's news about Mooneyham's court case against Goffman.

"Mooneyham ended his case on Saturday morning," Oscar informed him. "He presented it perfectly. The Goffman boys were confident at the beginning, but now they're scared. Mooneyham destroyed their chief witness, a scientist who claimed that there is no direct link between Maxatil and the plaintiff's breast cancer, by producing evidence of bad work he'd done twenty years ago. I've never seen a witness so thoroughly humbled."

"Beautiful, beautiful," Clay kept saying.

"Here's the best part," Oscar continued. "I've moved into the hotel where the Goffman people are staying and I see them at breakfast and in the bar late at night. They know who I am, and their lawyer, a man named Fleet, offered to buy me a drink soon after their chief witness had been destroyed by Mooneyham. He told me that Goffman was thinking about settling with Mooneyham. They're sure that the jury is on Mooneyham's side, and they're very frightened. Fleet wanted to know whether we would be ready to settle for $100,000 for each of our twenty-six thousand plaintiffs. Think about it, Clay. That's $2.6 billion! It wasn't an offer, but it's a first step. As we have the biggest class-action lawsuit against them, Goffman sent Fleet to talk to me. If we're willing to settle for $100,000 each, then Goffman can predict their total future costs."

"When do you see him again?"

"We agreed to meet outside the courtroom in an hour's time, just before the trial starts again."

"Call me as soon as you can."

"Don't worry, chief. How are the broken bones?"

"Much better now."

♦

Just before midday, Rebecca phoned Clay to say that she was on her way up to see him. Minutes later, she walked into his room and appeared shocked at the sight of him. She kissed him on the cheek, between bruises.

"You look awful," she said. Her eyes were filled with tears.

"Can I ask you a question?" Clay said.

"Of course."

"Where is your husband right now?"

"I'm not sure. São Paulo or Hong Kong maybe."

"Does he know you're here?"

"Of course not."

"What would he do if he knew you were here?"

"He'd be upset. I'm sure we'd fight."

"Would that be unusual?"

"It happens all the time, I'm afraid. Our marriage isn't working, Clay. I want to leave him."

Despite his wounds, Clay was having a wonderful day. Mooneyham's case against Goffman was going well, and now Rebecca wanted to leave her husband! The door to his room opened quietly and Ridley entered. She was at the foot of the bed, unnoticed, when she said, "Sorry to interrupt."

"Hi, Ridley," Clay said weakly.

The women gave each other looks more poisonous than snakebites. Ridley moved to the other side of the bed, directly opposite Rebecca, who kept her hand on Clay's bruised arm. "Ridley, this is Rebecca, Rebecca, this is Ridley," Clay said, then gave serious consideration to pulling the sheets over his head and pretending to be dead.

Neither smiled. Ridley reached over a few inches and began gently rubbing Clay's right arm. As there was nothing anybody could say for a few seconds, Clay nodded to his left and said, "She's an old friend," then to his right, and said, "She's a new friend." Both women at that moment felt annoyed at being referred to as just a friend.

"I believe we were at your wedding reception," Ridley said finally to Rebecca.

"Uninvited, if I remember correctly," Rebecca replied.

Both women stared at each other, neither of them moving an inch, and Clay was praying for a nurse to arrive. He didn't want a catfight to start over his bed. But the halls were silent and both women were stroking his arms.

Rebecca looked away first. She had no choice—she did have a husband.

"I guess I'll be going," she sighed.

She left the room slowly, not wishing to give Ridley the idea that she was surrendering any territory.

As soon as the door was closed, Ridley moved away to the

window, where she stood for a long time, staring at nothing. Clay looked through a newspaper, completely unconcerned with her or what she might be feeling.

"You love her, don't you?" Ridley said, still looking out of the window, trying to appear wounded.

"Who?"

"Rebecca."

"No. She's just an old friend."

She turned to him suddenly. "I'm not stupid, Clay!"

"I didn't say you were," Clay calmly replied, not taking his eyes from the newspaper.

She grabbed her purse and marched angrily out of the room.

A few minutes later, Oscar called on his cell phone outside the courtroom.

"I've heard a rumor that Mooneyham turned down an offer of $10 million this morning," he said.

"Did Fleet tell you this?"

"No. We didn't meet."

"What's happening at the moment?"

"Another Goffman witness is being questioned—a female professor who's criticizing the government study on Maxatil. Mooneyham is sharpening his knives. It should be ugly."

"Do you believe the rumor?"

"I'm not sure what to believe. The Wall Street boys seem excited about it. They want a settlement because they think that's the best way to predict costs. I'll call you back later."

There were three possible results in Flagstaff, and the first two would make Clay a very rich man again. If Mooneyham won, Goffman would have to settle with all the other plaintiffs to avoid years of lawsuits and bad publicity. Alternatively, a mid-trial settlement would probably mean a national compensation plan for all plaintiffs. Thinking about the third possibility brought back the sharp pains in Clay's head and legs: if Mooneyham lost

92

his case, Clay would have to prepare for his own trial in D.C.

A nurse closed the curtains and turned off the lights and the TV. When she was gone, Clay rested the phone on his stomach, pulled the sheets over his head, and waited.

◆

The next morning, Clay was taken back to surgery for some minor adjustments to the pins and screws in his legs. He returned to his room just after noon, and slept for three hours. Paulette, who had heard from Jonah about Clay's situation and had flown back from London to see him, was waiting when he finally woke up.

"Any word from Mulrooney?" Clay asked, with a thick tongue.

"He called to say the trial was going well," Paulette reported.

She adjusted his bed and pillow, gave him water and, just before she left, handed Clay an overnight envelope, unopened.

It was from Patton French. A handwritten note expressed his best wishes for a speedy recovery. The attached letter was from Helen Warshaw. There were now even more people on the list of people suing the members of the Dyloft Plaintiffs' Guidance Committee.

Ridley finally came in on her way home from the gym. She brought him some books and magazines, and tried to look concerned. After a few minutes she said, "Clay, the decorator called. I need to return to Mustique."

"When?" he asked.

"Tomorrow, maybe. If the plane is available."

"Sure. I'll call the pilots."

Clay felt pleased. Getting Ridley out of town would make his life easier. She was of no benefit around the hospital.

"Thanks," she said, then sat in the chair and began reading a magazine. After thirty minutes, she stood up, kissed Clay on the forehead, and disappeared.

The detective was next. Three men from Reedsburg had been arrested early Sunday morning outside a bar in Hagerstown, Maryland. He showed Clay color photos of the men—all rough-looking characters—but Clay couldn't identify any of them.

Oscar Mulrooney called at 9:30 P.M. Mooneyham had had another good day in court, and everybody was exhausted.

"Will Goffman ask again for a settlement?" Clay asked.

"No, but it should be a long night. There's a rumor that Goffman might try one last expert witness tomorrow. Mooneyham refuses to talk to them. He seems confident of winning the case."

♦

At 9 A.M. the next morning, Roger Redding surprised the court by announcing that the defense had no more witnesses. Mooneyham slowly got to his feet, scratched his head, frowned at Redding and said to the judge, "If they've finished, then so are we."

The judge explained to the jurors that there would be a one-hour break while he discussed matters with the two lawyers. When they returned, they would hear the closing arguments, and then at lunchtime they, the jury, could go away and start discussing the case.

With everyone else, Oscar Mulrooney ran into the hallway, cell phone in his hand. Clay was asleep when Oscar called. There was no answer in Clay's hospital room. Clay had been taken away to another department and had left his cell phone on his bed.

Oscar finally managed to contact Clay a few hours later.

"Where have you been?" he demanded.

"Don't ask," Clay replied with annoyance at having been away from his phone for so long.

"Goffman surrendered this morning," Oscar said. "They tried to settle, but Mooneyham refused to listen. Everything happened real fast after that. Closing arguments began around ten, I guess. The jury left to consider the case at exactly noon."

"The jury already has the case?" Clay asked, shouting with excitement.

"They *had* the case."

"What?"

"They had the case. It's done. They considered it for three hours and found in favor of Goffman. I'm sorry, Clay. Everybody here is in shock."

"No."

"I'm afraid so."

"Tell me you're lying, Oscar."

"I wish I were. I don't know what happened. Nobody does. Redding made a very good closing speech, but I watched the jurors. I still thought they were on Mooneyham's side."

"Dale Mooneyham lost a case?"

"Not just any case, Clay. He lost our case."

"But how?"

"I don't know. I would have bet all my money on Mooneyham."

"We just did."

"I'm sorry."

"Listen, Oscar, I'm lying here in bed, all alone. I'm closing my eyes now and I want you to just talk to me. Tell me something."

"After the trial, Fleet and a couple of other guys from Goffman came up to me and told me that they were looking forward to the next trial which would be in D.C., against Mr. Clay Carter, the King of the Torts, who, as we all know, has never tried a tort case in his life. What could I say? They had just beaten an experienced lawyer like Mooneyham."

"Our cases are worthless, Oscar."

"*They* certainly think so. They told me they wouldn't offer a single cent for any Maxatil case anywhere in the country. They want trials."

Clay kept Oscar on the phone for over an hour, as his unlit room grew dark. Oscar explained in detail the closing arguments; he described the high tension of waiting for the jury's decision, and the shock on the plaintiff's face—a dying woman whose lawyer wouldn't take the $10 million that Goffman was rumored to be offering. Mooneyham, who hadn't lost a case for so long that he had forgotten *how* to lose, demanded that the jury explain in writing how they had reached their decision. And there was the shock on the Goffman side when they heard the jury's final decision.

Oscar ended his story by saying, "I'm going to the bar now."

Clay called a nurse and asked for a sleeping pill.


## Chapter 16   Return to Sanity

Eleven days later, Clay was finally released from the hospital. Paulette pushed his wheelchair out of the hospital to a rented van driven by Oscar. Fifteen minutes later, they rolled him into his town house and locked the door. Paulette and Miss Glick had turned the downstairs into a temporary bedroom. His phones and computer had been moved to a folding table near his bed. His clothes were piled neatly on plastic shelves by the fireplace.

For the first two hours he was home, he read mail and financial reports, but only what Paulette allowed him to see. Most of what had been printed about Clay was kept away from him. Later, after a short sleep, he sat at the kitchen table with Paulette and Oscar and announced that it was time for serious discussion.

Two days earlier, Oscar had unwillingly agreed to go to New York to meet with Helen Warshaw and basically to beg for her mercy. His boss didn't want to file for bankruptcy but, if pushed too hard by Ms. Warshaw, he would have no choice. She had been unimpressed. Clay was a member of a group of lawyers with a combined value, in her opinion, of $1.5 billion. She could not allow him to pay less compensation than the other lawyers in the group. Plus, she wasn't in a settling mood. The trial would be an important one and she planned to enjoy every moment of it.

Gradually, over the past few weeks, the word *bankruptcy* had been used more and more until, among Clay's staff, it had become part of everyone's vocabulary. If the firm went bankrupt, Clay would lose his office, his car, his boat, his private jet, and his house on Mustique. However, he would not have to fight Goffman in court, the unhappy Hanna plaintiffs would be forced to settle and, most importantly, Helen Warshaw would not be able to take him to court.

After discussing bankruptcy for a few hours, Oscar left for the office and Paulette wheeled Clay outside for a cup of green tea with honey.

"I have two things to say," she said, sitting very close and staring at him. "First, I'm going to give you some of my money."

"No, you're not."

"Yes, I am. You made me rich when you didn't have to. It's not my fault you're a stupid white boy who's lost everything, but I still love you. I'm going to help you, Clay."

"Can you believe all this, Paulette?"

"No, it's beyond belief, but it's true. It's happened. And things will get much worse before they get better. Don't read the papers, Clay. Please. Promise me that."

"Don't worry."

"I'm going to help you. If you lose everything, I'll be around to make sure you're OK."

"I don't know what to say."

"Say nothing."

They held hands and Clay fought back tears. A moment passed.

"Number two," she said. "I've been talking to Rebecca. She's afraid to see you because she might get caught. She has a new cell phone which her husband knows nothing about. She gave me the number. She wants you to call her this afternoon. Her husband's out of town. I'll leave in a few minutes."

♦

Rebecca and Jason Myers had decided to end their marriage. At first he had wanted to delay the divorce, but he also preferred to work eighteen hours a day, whether he was in D.C., New York, or Hong Kong. His firm had offices in thirty-two cities, and he had clients around the world. Work was more important than anything else. He had simply left her, with no apologies and with no plans to change his ways. The divorce papers would be filed in two days. Rebecca was already packing her bags. Jason would keep their property; she didn't know where she was going to live. In less than a year of marriage, they had saved little money. He earned $800,000 a year, but she wanted none of his salary.

According to Rebecca, her parents had not caused any problems. They hadn't had the chance. Myers didn't like them, which was no surprise, and Clay suspected that one reason why he preferred to work in Hong Kong was because it was so far away from the Van Horns.

Both had a reason to run. Clay wouldn't, under any circumstances, remain in D.C. He wanted to go somewhere where people didn't know him. For the first time in her life, Rebecca just wanted to get away—away from a bad marriage, away from her family, away from the country club and the awful people who went there, away from the pressures of making money and acquiring possessions.

Rebecca spent the night with Clay and decided not to leave. Over coffee the next morning, Clay began with Tequila Watson and Tarvan and told her everything.

Paulette and Oscar returned from the office with more bad news. The homeowners in Reedsburg were being encouraged to file a lawsuit against Clay for mishandling the Hanna case. In total, six lawsuits had been filed against Clay, all by the same attorney, who was actively looking for more. Clay's office was organizing a settlement plan to be put in front of the judge in the Hanna bankruptcy.

In addition to this, Helen Warshaw wanted to record the evidence of several of the Dyloft plaintiffs. Urgency was required because they were dying, and their video evidence would be important to the trial, which was expected in about a year. Clay agreed to the schedule suggested by Ms. Warshaw, although he had no plans to attend the recording of evidence himself.

Under pressure from Oscar, Clay finally agreed to reduce the number of staff at his firm. A letter to the Maxatil clients was also planned and written, in which Clay explained that, after the Mooneyham trial in Flagstaff, it would be almost impossible to prove a link between the drug and cancer. Goffman wasn't willing to consider an out-of-court settlement, and Clay wasn't well enough to prepare for a long trial. He was therefore releasing each client from their contract, and wished them luck in any future fight against Goffman with another law firm.

There were a hundred other details on Oscar's checklist, but Clay was tired.

"Do you want me to stay tonight?" Paulette asked.

"No, Rebecca's here."

"You love trouble, don't you?"

"She's filing for divorce tomorrow."

"What about the Russian girl?"

"I've finished with her."

For the next week, Clay never left his town house. Rebecca packed all of Ridley's things away in the basement and moved in some of her own stuff, although Clay warned her that he was soon going to lose the house. She cooked him wonderful meals and nursed him whenever he needed it. They watched old movies until midnight, then slept late every morning.

◆

The last lawyer to enter Clay's life was Mark Munson, a bankruptcy expert whom Crittle had found. Clay discovered that in the seventeen months since he had left OPD, he had earned $121 million in fees, but most of this had been spent. He had also earned $7.1 million trading in Ackerman shares, but this would all have to be paid back. "If you hide money, you go to jail," Munson warned him.

Clay was left with approximately $19 million. However, he now had twenty-six former clients suing him over Dyloft, the Hanna class-action plaintiffs were getting organized, and the consequences of Maxatil would be nasty and expensive. None of these expenses could be accurately predicted.

"When it ends," Munson said, "you'll have no money, but at least you won't owe anything."

"Thanks," Clay said with a bitter smile.

After two hours with Munson and Crittle, the kitchen table was covered with paper: all that was left of the past seventeen months of his life. He was ashamed of his greed and his stupidity. It was sickening what the money had done to him.

The thought of leaving helped him survive each day.

◆

Ridley called from Mustique with the alarming news that a FOR SALE sign had appeared in front of "their" house.

"That's because it's now for sale," Clay said.

"I don't understand."

"Come home and I'll explain it to you."

"Is there trouble?"

"There is."

After a long pause, she said, "I prefer to stay here."

"Fine. Stay in the house until it sells. I don't care."

♦

Rodney found his old friend sitting by the window.

"How are the bones?" he asked, sitting beside him.

"Healing nicely."

"How's your head?"

"No additional brain damage."

"How's your soul?"

"Surviving."

"Paulette says you're leaving."

"For some time, anyway. I'll file for bankruptcy next week, and I won't be around here when it happens. Paulette has a flat in London that I can use for a few months. We'll hide there."

"You can't avoid a bankruptcy?"

"No. There are too many good claims against us. Remember our first Dyloft plaintiff, Ted Worley?"

"Sure."

"He died yesterday. I didn't kill him, but I didn't protect him either. His case in front of a jury is worth $5 million. There are twenty-six other cases similar to his. I'm going to London."

"Clay, I want to help."

"I'm not taking your money. I've had this conversation twice with Paulette and once with Jonah. You made your money and you were smart enough to get out at the right time. I wasn't."

"You didn't have to give us $10 million. We're giving some back."

"No."

"Yes. The three of us have talked about it. We'll wait until the bankruptcy is over, then each of us will transfer money to your account. A gift."

"You earned that money, Rodney. Keep it."

"Nobody earns $10 million in six months, Clay. You might

101

win it, steal it, or see it drop out of the sky, but nobody *earns* money like that. It's ridiculous. I'm giving some back. So are Paulette and Jonah."

"How are the kids?"

"You're changing the subject."

"Yes, I'm changing the subject."

So they talked about kids, and old friends at OPD, and old clients and cases there. They sat on the front steps until after dark, when Rebecca arrived and it was time for dinner.

◆

Paulette and Rodney drove Clay and Rebecca to Reagan National Airport, where Clay's Gulfstream jet sat very close to the spot where he had first seen it. As they were leaving for at least six months, there was a lot of luggage, especially Rebecca's. Clay, who had sold most of his possessions, was traveling light. He could walk fairly easily, but he was still too weak to carry anything. Rodney acted as his porter.

Clay climbed the steps of his jet for one last journey, said goodbye to Paulette and Rodney, thanked them both, and promised to call within days. When the door was shut, Clay pulled the shades down over the windows so that he would see none of Washington when they lifted off.

To Rebecca, the jet was a terrible symbol of the destructive power of greed. She was looking forward to the tiny flat in London, where no one knew them and no one cared what they wore, drove, bought, ate, or where they worked, shopped, or went on vacation. She wasn't coming home. She had fought with her parents for the last time.

Clay wanted nothing more than two good legs and a fresh start. He was surviving one of the biggest disasters in the history of American law, and it was further and further behind him. He had Rebecca now, and nothing else mattered.

Somewhere over Newfoundland, they unfolded the sofa and fell asleep under the covers.

# ACTIVITIES

## Chapters 1–3

*Before you read*

**1** Read the Introduction and answer these questions.

    **a** What are most John Grisham stories about?

    **b** How is *The King of Torts* different from his other legal thrillers?

**2** Look at the Word List at the back of the book and answer these questions.

    **a** Which words describe people's roles and jobs?

    **b** Which words relate to trials and courtrooms?

    **c** Which words relate to the human body, its workings, and its problems?

**3** Discuss these questions with another student.

    **a** Which of these words describe lawyers in your country? Give examples to support your views.

        affordable   intelligent   moral   popular

    **b** If you were a lawyer and could accept one of the following cases, which would you choose? Why?

        • An old woman wants to sue the local authority because she has stepped into a hole in the sidewalk and broken her ankle.

        • An old man wants to sue a tobacco company because smoking has given him lung cancer.

        • A young woman wants to sue her doctor because the drugs he gave her have made her seriously ill.

*While you read*

**4** Finish these sentences with the following names.

    Jonah   Senator Ian Ludkin   Max Pace   Washad Porter
    Adelfa Pumphrey   Rodney   Paulette Tullos   Bennett Van Horn
    Rebecca   Tequila Watson   Talmadge X

    **a** ............................................ murders

        ............................................ 's son.

    **b** ............................................ like Clay, is a lawyer at the OPD.

103

**c** ........................................... works with drug addicts.

**d** Clay doesn't like ........................................... .

**e** ........................................... works at the OPD but isn't a lawyer.

**f** ........................................... has committed a similar crime to Clay's client.

**g** Clay rejects an offer to work for ........................................... .

**h** ........................................... wants to stop seeing Clay.

**i** ........................................... went to law school with Clay.

**j** Clay's life is changed by ........................................... 's offer.

*After you read*

**5** How are these places important in this part of the story?

   **a** an alley near Lamont Street    **e** Clean Streets

   **b** the Criminal Justice Center    **f** Abe's Place

   **c** Deliverance Camp    **g** the Willard Hotel

   **d** the Potomac Country Club    **h** Connecticut Avenue

**6** Discuss these questions with another student.

   **a** What is unusual about the murders committed by Tequila Watson and Washad Porter?

   **b** How do Bennett Van Horn and Clay feel about each other? Why?

   **c** What is the connection between an unnamed pharmaceutical company and Tequila Watson?

   **d** Is Clay right to accept Max Pace's offer? Why (not)?

## Chapters 4–6

*Before you read*

**7** If you knew that a pharmaceutical company was responsible for the death of someone in your family, would you

   • accept a lot of money in compensation and ask no questions?

   • refuse compensation and try to take the pharmaceutical company to court?

*While you read*

**8** Circle the correct endings to these sentences.

**a** Clay and Jonah *are colleagues at the OPD / share the same address.*

**b** Seven people *have been killed as a result of Tarvan / become clients of Clay's new law firm.*

**c** Dyloft helps people who have trouble with their *joints / bladders.*

**d** Clay doesn't tell the others in his firm about *Max Pace / Dyloft.*

**e** Patton French wants *Clay to stop working on the Dyloft case / to work with Clay.*

**f** Clay makes a profit of $6 million when *he buys back his shares in Ackerman Labs / Philo Products buys Ackerman Labs.*

**g** In New York, Clay becomes interested in *other lawsuits against Ackerman Labs / a Pennsylvanian cement company.*

**h** Ackerman Labs *agrees to pay compensation / decides to fight the case in court.*

*After you read*

**9** How does Clay feel, and why,

    **a** after talking to the last Tarvan clients?

    **b** after talking to Max Pace in his office?

    **c** after telephoning Ted Worley?

    **d** after seeing the *Wall Street Journal*?

    **e** after reading about Tequila Watson?

    **f** when he meets Patton French for the first time?

    **g** the morning after speaking to Max Pace in Georgetown?

    **h** after talking to Rex Crittle?

    **i** after talking to Wes Saulsberry?

    **j** after telephoning Rebecca?

**10** Work with another student. Have this conversation.

    *Student A:* You are Clay. You want Rodney to leave the OPD and join your new law firm. Tell him why, but don't say anything about Max Pace.

    *Student B:* You are Rodney. You are happy at the OPD. Tell

Clay why you don't want to leave.

**11** Discuss these statements. What do you think?

   **a** The more successful Clay is, the less likeable he becomes.

   **b** Ted Worley is quite right to be angry with Clay.

## Chapters 7–9

*Before you read*

   **12** What will happen when Clay next meets Rebecca? Why?

*While you read*

   **13** In which order do these happen? Number them 1–10.

     **a** People are scared by an advertisement. .....

     **b** Patton French refuses to join Clay in a lawsuit. .....

     **c** Max Pace visits Clay on a Caribbean island. .....

     **d** Clay flies to Arizona. .....

     **e** Rebecca gets married. .....

     **f** Clay meets the U.S. President. .....

     **g** Clay has dinner with a beautiful foreigner. .....

     **h** Jonah and Paulette leave Clay's firm. .....

     **i** Clay hides from angry clients. .....

     **j** Clay is criticized in the newspapers. .....

*After you read*

   **14** Who is speaking and who to? Who or what are they talking about?

     **a** "I'm looking for a young woman."

     **b** "You still love her, don't you?"

     **c** "I'd like to break his neck."

     **d** "Don't cause any trouble."

     **e** "Be brave."

     **f** "This could be bigger than Dyloft."

     **g** "Juries love him."

     **h** "I've shocked them before, I'll shock them again."

     **i** "I didn't like it six months ago, and I don't like it now."

     **j** "Mass torts are a fraud."

   **15** What do these people think of Clay's professional abilities? Which of them do you agree with most? Why?

     Max Pace   Patton French   Dale Mooneyham

## Chapters 10–12

*Before you read*

**16** What problems might Clay have in the next part of the story with:

   **a** the Maxatil case?

   **b** the Hanna Portland Cement Company?

   **c** Rebecca?

   **d** the FBI?

   **e** his accountant?

   **f** Dyloft clients?

*While you read*

**17** Are these sentences true (✓) or false (✗)?

   **a** The Hanna brothers are popular with their workers. .....

   **b** Rodney leaves the law firm because it doesn't need him any more. .....

   **c** Patton French thinks Dale Mooneyham is a good lawyer. .....

   **d** The Hanna brothers deny that their company produced bad cement. .....

   **e** The FBI ask Clay about Tarvan. .....

   **f** Clay feels happy after his meeting with Rebecca. .....

   **g** Helen Warshaw sues Clay, Patton French, and Ackerman Labs. .....

   **h** Clay writes a letter of apology to Ted Worley. .....

   **i** Clay lies to the FBI on their second visit. .....

   **j** Zack Battle advises Clay to sue Max Pace. .....

*After you read*

**18** Look at your answers to Question 16. Were you right? Why (not)?

**19** Find the correct endings (1–10) to these sentences:

   **a** Marcus Hanna is shocked because his company .....

   **b** Rodney leaves the firm because he .....

   **c** Patton French is unwilling to sue Goffman because he .....

   **d** Max Pace is wanted by the FBI because he .....

   **e** Rex Crittle is worried because Clay's firm .....

   **f** Mrs. Worley contacts Helen Warshaw because she .....

**g** Reporters want to speak to Clay because Clay      …..
**h** Clay laughs and jokes with his staff because he      …..
**i** Clay hopes that Max Pace is hiding in Europe because he      …..
**j** Tequila Watson writes to Clay because he      …..

   **1)** wants to hide his true feelings.
   **2)** thinks it might be difficult to link breast cancer to Maxatil.
   **3)** wants better compensation for her husband.
   **4)** doesn't have enough insurance to cover the costs of the lawsuit.
   **5)** has made illegal profits.
   **6)** wants Clay to apologize to Pumpkin's family.
   **7)** is being sued.
   **8)** doesn't have any insurance.
   **9)** doesn't want the FBI to know the truth about his Ackerman shares.
   **10)** wants to spend more time with his family.

**20** Discuss these questions with another student. What do you think?

   **a** What is Clay's biggest problem in this part of the story— the Hanna Portland Cement Company case, the FBI, Helen Warshaw, or the Maxatil case? Why?
   **b** Do you hope Helen Warshaw wins her case against Clay and the other Dyloft lawyers? Why (not)?

### Chapters 13–16

*Before you read*

**21** How will the story end for Clay, do you think?

*While you read*

**22** Check (✓) the correct answer.

   **a** Why does the Hanna Portland Cement Company go bankrupt?
      **1)** Clay wants too much money.      …..
      **2)** Too many plaintiffs are claiming compensation.      …..

**b** How does Clay feel after Rebecca's visit to his office?

    **1)** More optimistic about the future of their
       relationship. .....

    **2)** Less worried about the bad publicity about him. .....

**c** Why does the judge ask Clay to leave Arizona?

    **1)** Mooneyham disapproves of Clay. .....

    **2)** Clay has broken the judge's rules. .....

**d** After reading *Newsweek*, what does Clay regret?

    **1)** Not having reduced his fees with the cement
       company. .....

    **2)** Having become a lawyer. .....

**e** What does Patton French advise Clay?

    **1)** To drop the lawsuit against Goffman. .....

    **2)** Not to represent his clients in court. .....

**f** Why is Clay is attacked in the street?

    **1)** Because of his handling of the Dyloft case. .....

    **2)** Because of his handling of the cement company
       case. .....

**g** Who visits him in the hospital?

    **1)** a former colleague. .....

    **2)** Patton French. .....

**h** Who is pleased by the jury's decision?

    **1)** Clay. .....

    **2)** Goffman. .....

**i** How does her divorce from Jason Myers leave
  Rebecca?

    **1)** Rich. .....

    **2)** Homeless. .....

**j** How does Clay feel at the end of the story?

    **1)** Optimistic about the future. .....

    **2)** Worried about his debts. .....

*After you read*

**23** Who do these sentences describe, and why?

  **a** They walk angrily out of a meeting.

  **b** He refuses to answer the phone.

**c** He refuses to shake Clay's hand.

**d** They cover a car with cement.

**e** He laughs at Clay in the hospital.

**f** He wants to pretend to be dead.

**g** His client is shocked by the jury's decision.

**h** She insists on a trial.

**i** She prefers to stay in the Caribbean.

**j** They offer Clay financial assistance.

**24** How do these people feel about Clay at the end of the story, and why? Discuss your answers with another student.

| | | | |
|---|---|---|---|
| **a** | his Maxatil clients | **e** | the cement company plaintiffs |
| **b** | Patton French | **f** | Rebecca |
| **c** | Oscar Mulrooney | **g** | Ridley |
| **d** | Paulette and Rodney | **h** | Mrs. Worley |

**25** Work with another student. Have this conversation, in London.

*Student A:* You are Max Pace. You have another money-making plan for Clay. Tell him about it. Try to persuade him to join you.

*Student B:* You are Clay. Tell Pace what you think of his idea.

**26** Discuss these questions with another student.

**a** Does the story end as you expected? Why (not)?

**b** Who do you feel most sorry for at the end of the story? Why?

**c** What were Clay's biggest mistakes? What lessons should he learn from them?

## Writing

**27** You are an inspector for the Justice Department. You have investigated complaints about Clay Carter's activities and behavior as a lawyer, and talked to witnesses. Should Clay be allowed to work as a lawyer again? Why (not)? Write your report.

**28** You are Rebecca (Chapter 2). Write Clay a letter, explaining why you don't want to see him again.

**29** You are Clay. You can't decide whether to accept Max Pace's offer (Chapter 3). Write a letter to a close friend, explaining why the decision is so difficult.

**30** You are Dale Mooneyham (Chapter 15). You are not happy with the jury's decision in the Maxatil case and you want another trial. Write to the Justice Department and explain why.

**31** You are one of the jurors in the Maxatil case (Chapter 15). Write to Dale Mooneyham, explaining how and why you and the other jurors reached your decision.

**32** Write about the importance in the story of Tarvan, Dyloft, Maxatil, and bad cement. How did each of them benefit and/or damage Clay's career? Which of them damaged his career the most? How?

**33** You are Paulette (Chapter 8). Email Clay, explaining why you don't want to work for him any more.

**34** How are these people important in the story? Write a paragraph about: Tequila Watson, Ted Worley, Helen Warshaw, and Ridley.

**35** You are Marcus Hanna (Chapter 13). Write an open letter to your workers explaining why they have lost their jobs.

**36** You are an influential retired judge. You are not happy about the behavior of mass tort lawyers in general. You want them to be less greedy in future and to make sure that plaintiffs benefit more from their lawsuits. Write a proposal explaining why you are unhappy with the present situation and making suggestions for improvements in future mass tort practice.

# WORD LIST

**arthritis** (n) a disease that causes pain and swelling in the joints of your body

**bladder** (n) the part of your body where urine is stored before it leaves your body

**briefcase** (n) a flat case used for carrying books and papers for work

**class action** (n) a lawsuit that is brought to court by many plaintiffs at the same time

**colleague** (n) someone you work with

**committee** (n) a group of people who meet regularly to do a particular job or make decisions

**corporate** (adj) relating to a corporation

**counselor** (n) someone whose job is to advise people who have problems

**damages** (n pl) money that someone must pay to another person for harming them or their property

**entitle** (v) to give someone moral or legal permission to do or have something

**file** (v) to start a legal process in the official way

**handcuffs** (n pl) two metal rings joined by a chain, used for holding a prisoner's wrists together. If you *handcuff* prisoners, you put handcuffs on their wrists.

**hormone** (n) a substance produced by your body which helps it to develop or grow

**lawsuit** (n) a problem or complaint that someone brings to a court of law

**litigate** (v) to take a legal case to a court of law

**malignant** (adj) containing cancer cells

**menopause** (n) the time in a woman's life, usually when she is about fifty years old, when she stops producing eggs and can no longer have children

**paralegal** (n) a person whose job is to assist lawyers in their work

**pharmaceuticals** (n/pl) drugs produced by a company that